THIS I DO BELIEVE

THIS

I DO BELIEVE

BY

DAVID E. LILIENTHAL

HARPER & BROTHERS PUBLISHERS

NEW YORK

THIS I DO BELIEVE

Gen'l.

THIS BOOK IS DEDICATED

TO

NANCY AND DAVID

AND TO THE YOUNG MEN AND WOMEN

OF THEIR GENERATION

OF FREE AMERICANS

D. E. L.
H. M. L.

CONTENTS

"*This I Do Carry In My Head, Senator....*"

a report by Alfred Friendly

(The publishers have obtained permission from Alfred Friendly and the Washington Post *to reprint the following excerpt from Mr. Friendly's report of February 4, 1947 of David E. Lilienthal's dramatic declaration of his faith in democracy before a Joint Congressional Committee.)*

(WASHINGTON, FEB. 4)

For more than a week, Senator Kenneth D. McKellar (D., Tenn.) has used the hearings of the Joint Congressional Committee on Atomic Energy as a forum in which to attack David E. Lilienthal. The committee is considering the confirmation of the former TVA head in his new post of Atomic Energy Commission chairman.

McKellar's line of questioning has been apparently designed to portray Lilienthal as a Communist.

Yesterday, on a side excursion, McKellar demanded to know TVA's production cost of a ton of ammonium nitrate.

Lilienthal said the figures were available, that he would obtain them, but that he did not carry them in

ix

his head. McKellar professed to find this answer in itself, evidence of Lilienthal's gross incompetence. He repeatedly requoted it, with heavy sarcasm.

Later, back on his original tack, McKellar snapped, "The truth is that your sympathies are very leftist."

"The truth is," Lilienthal answered, "that an answer to that assertion cannot be made in terms of 'yes or no.' "

"Well, what are your convictions on Communist doctrine?" McKellar persisted.

The witness, who until yesterday had shown no signs of emotion or anger under McKellar's barrage, suddenly wheeled in his chair to face his antagonist. He said, in a voice which was low, but electric with fervor:

"This I DO carry in my head, Senator.

"I will do my best to make it clear. My convictions are not so much concerned with what I am against as what I am for; and that excludes a lot of things automatically.

"Traditionally, democracy has been an affirmative doctrine rather than merely a negative one.

"I believe—and I conceive the Constitution of the United States to rest, as does religion, upon the fundamental proposition of the integrity of the individual; and that all government and all private institutions must be designed to promote and protect and defend the integrity and the dignity of the individual; that that is the essential meaning of the Constitution and the Bill of Rights, as it is essentially the meaning of religion.

"Any form of government, therefore, and any other institutions which make men means rather than ends, which exalt the state or any other institutions above the importance of men, which place arbitrary power over men as a fundamental tenet of government are contrary to that conception, and, therefore, I am deeply opposed to them.

"The communistic philosophy as well as the communistic form of government falls within this category, for their fundamental tenet is quite to the contrary. The fundamental tenet of communism is that the state is an end in itself, and that therefore the powers which the state exercises over the individual are without any ethical standard to limit them.

"That I deeply disbelieve.

"It is very easy simply to say that one is not a Communist. And, of course, if despite my record it is necessary for me to state this very affirmatively, then it is a great disappointment to me.

"It is very easy to talk about being against communism. It is equally important to believe those things which provide a satisfying and effective alternative. Democracy is that satisfying, affirmative alternative.

"Its hope in the world is that it is an affirmative belief, rather than being simply a belief against something else and nothing more.

"One of the tenets of democracy that grows out of this central core of a belief that the individual comes first, that all men are the children of God and that their personalities are therefore sacred, is a deep belief in civil liberties and their protection, and a repugnance to anyone who would steal from a human being that which

is most precious to him—his good name—either by
imputing things to him by innuendo or by insinuation.
And it is especially an unhappy circumstance that occasionally that is done in the name of democracy. This, I
think, can tear our country apart and destroy it if we
carry it further.

"I deeply believe in the capacity of democracy to surmount any trials that may lie ahead, provided only that
we practice it in our daily lives.

"And among the things we must practice is this: that
while we seek fervently to ferret out the subversive and
anti-democratic forces in the country, we do not at the
same time, by hysteria, by resort to innuendo, and
smears, and other unfortunate tactics, besmirch the very
cause that we believe in, and cause a separation among
our people—cause one group and one individual to hate
another, based on mere attacks, mere unsubstantiated
attacks upon their loyalty.

"I want also to add that part of my conviction is
based on my training as an Anglo-American common
lawyer. It is the very basis and the great heritage of the
English people to this country, which we have maintained, that we insist on the strictest rules of credibility
of witnesses and on the avoidance of hearsay, and that
gossip shall be excluded, in the courts of justice. And
that, too, is an essential of our democracy.

"Whether by administrative agencies acting arbi-
trarily against business organizations, or whether by in-
vestigating activities of legislative branches, whenever
those principles fail, those principles of the protection

of an individual and his good name against besmirch-
ment by gossip, hearsay, and the statements of witnesses
who are not subject to cross-examination—then, too, we
have failed in carrying forward our ideals in respect to
democracy.

"This I deeply believe."

The pin-drop silence which had obtained throughout
Lilienthal's remarks lasted several moments more.

Then Senator McMahon (D., Conn.) said in a quiet
voice, "That was the statement of a very real American."

There was still another period of complete silence.
Then McKellar shuffled his papers and resumed, "Mr.
Lilienthal, while you were head of the TVA, did you
have any Communists in your employ?" . . .

Author's Note

THIS is a book of democratic faith.

What I have here written is a statement of the essentials of democracy as I understand them, and the reasons for my faith in those precepts. The practical support for the affirmations that form the theme and body of this credo have been drawn, for the most part, from my own experiences as an American public servant.

The idea that there should be such a book, as well as its theme and title, were suggested by my wife. Without her considerable help the book would not have been possible. And as a consequence of a collaboration that goes back over the more than twenty-five years of our married life, there is hardly an idea discussed in this book that we have not talked over together during that period, nor a page of the writing on which I have not had the benefit of her judgment and the stimulus of her own firm belief in these principles.

I wish also to record my great indebtedness to Gordon R. Clapp, Chairman of the TVA, for many helpful hours of discussion of a number of the problems of democratic principle and practical action about which I have expressed myself in this book.

DAVID E. LILIENTHAL

Washington, D. C.
July 8, 1949

Foreword: Where Does Democracy Stand Today?

WHERE does democracy stand today, here at home and in other parts of the world? Has a living democracy made headway in the past ten years, or is it losing ground in the world, and in the United States? I do not mean the mere expression of democracy in fine, eloquent words but the reality, the words as they are translated into the everyday life of everyday people.

What about the future? What are the prospects for the survival and the strengthening of a healthy creative democracy, one capable of standing up under rough handling in a very tough world, and yet with a spiritual force that will appeal to the deepest aspirations and hopes of men?

I know of no more important questions than these.

We need badly to take a good hard realistic look at our own American balance sheet of democratic assets and liabilities, for the fact is, as every American who is honest with himself must recognize, that for at least the last twenty years the trend in the world has been away from democracy, as we understand it and as we seek to practice it here at home.

We sorrow when we see that war and human insecurity
have withered those green shoots of democratic growth
that twenty years ago seemed healthful and promising in
many countries now enslaved. We need, therefore, to be
vigilant and alive about American democracy, and
above all, sternly and honestly critical. The fate of individualism throughout the world depends upon the
state of health of democracy here in the United States.
If individual freedom and individual opportunity
should falter and perish here in America, where in the
whole wide world will they survive?

The position of the United States in its relation to the
rest of the world has undergone a sudden and profound
change. It has rarely been the lot of men to live in the
very center of so great a change, and almost immediately
to be aware of it—and aware that they are participants
in its consequences. Just this, it seems to me, is what is
happening to us in the United States today.

This change has two quite different aspects. The
United States since the end of the War has become by
every measure the first nation of the world, not only first
in power and resources and in world influence, but first
in the vitality and the quality of the economic, political
and moral leadership she manifests.

The second aspect of this change is ominous and
deeply disturbing, and not without a majestic irony. For
at the high-tide of American power and leadership the
foundations of that power and leadership have quite
abruptly become the object of a sustained attack of the
broadest possible character, on a world-wide scale. This

assault by the Russian Communists is not superficial, concerned merely with traditional forms of competition for markets, or colonial areas, or commercial advantages. The spear is leveled at America's heart: her place in the respect and affection of peoples all over the world, not excluding her own citizens. The very attributes of American democracy that for more than a hundred years have expressed the highest aspirations both material and spiritual of the hundreds of millions of impoverished and oppressed peoples of Europe and Asia and Africa, are now challenged, challenged with bitterness, intensity and, one must admit, with no little effectiveness.

The attack is as thorough-going and comprehensive as it is fundamental. Nothing is spared: neither our accomplishments and standards in science nor in civil liberties, in architecture and the press, in music and competitive sports and military prowess. It is an attack on our motives, our institutions and the spirit of our people. The clear purpose is to bring world-wide contempt down upon our whole American democratic civilization. Nothing quite like this broad assault on us, even in time of actual warfare, has ever happened to this country. The question of democracy's standing in America is, therefore, more important than at any time in our history.

There are many words being written about democracy, and they are often eloquent and decorative and moving. But what do the words in the books, and the pleasant sounds in the speeches, mean for everyday life? How do the words look when they go to work? How do they translate for the men at the lathe in the factory, behind the farm tractor, in the science laboratory, in the union hall and church and university and book store and town council and bank and neighborhood meeting? Do the words about freedom and individual integrity pay off for them, or are they just words? What do democracy's books of account actually show? What are our strengths, our weaknesses? How does democracy measure up, in the everyday world of fact?

There are ways of doing an audit of this kind. It is the kind of measuring process that as a public servant I have tried to develop for my own guidance; in this book I have set down some of my conclusions. It is something every citizen can do, for himself; indeed, it is part of his job as a citizen.

Modern democracy is not just a form of government. It is not concerned solely with casting a ballot, or only with what goes on at the city hall or in Congress. When we say democracy is a way of life, we mean just that: a way of living each day, and not simply a matter of laws and government. Democracy is a way of looking at life. Democracy is concerned with fundamental principles of human conduct by which men judge what is good and what is evil, principles old and worn with centuries of thought and trial. What is new is not the principles. What is new is their application in our day to day living in the mid-twentieth century to a physical world that science and technology makes new.

So this stock-taking includes measuring against our democratic precepts what actually goes on about us in our

ordinary pursuits, and not alone what transpires in the
Senate, or at a Foreign Ministers Conference. Therefore
to the question: How is democracy getting along in this
country? The answer is found not only in Washington
but back home as well.

For almost twenty years it has been my job as a public
servant to try to translate what we say about democracy
into what we do. Day in day out I have had to face the
practical question: How can this or that thing get done,
not only for a democratic purpose but perhaps more important, in a democratic way?

My general conclusion about the advance of democracy
in the United States is sanguine and optimistic. I am convinced that in the main we have been making steady
progress. I believe that today the ground is firmer beneath our feet than it has ever been in the whole history
of the Republic.

I say this not as a scholar or a writer of surveys, but as
one who has been working at democracy, where the going
has been and still is rough. In my opinion, when the books
are balanced they will show that democracy is growing in
strength; in spite of some ugly danger spots, it seems to
me to be flourishing.

How can anyone possibly measure the progress or decline of democracy? How can we tell before it is too late,
whether we are actually marching ahead, up the long hard
road, or going down, down the tragic road toward
tyranny? Just counting the increase in number of inside
toilets, and television sets, and well-fed people certainly
is no measure in itself.

I believe that the progress or decline of democracy, in any particular set of circumstances, or at a particular time and place can be measured by finding out the answer to this question: What is happening to the individual? Since this is essentially an ethical and spiritual matter, the question is not solely one related to the individual's physical well-being.

Has opportunity for individual development been diminished or increased? Have individuals become more subject to arbitrary power of others, or are they less subject to arbitrary control—whether by government or employer or other forms of authority? Has the individual less or has he greater room to exercise his talents for the arts, for self-expression, for inquiry and thought? Are science and technology and business and government used as means for making the individual smaller, less important, while machines and corporations and government become ever more important? Or are science and technology and business and government tools that are consciously and deliberately developed and used to make the individual count for more, to aid him to further his own development, to enable him to do more and more for himself, according to his own talents, aspirations and capacities?

Democratic action, then, according to this kind of yardstick, is that which furthers the importance of the individual by methods that increase individual self-development, responsibility, and integrity. In subsequent chapters of this book I have developed this theme, and cited specific illustrations out of my own experience.

Democracy, unlike communism, is not a dogma, with all the answers coming down to us from a political or bureaucratic hierarchy. The essential ingredient of democracy is not doctrine but intelligence, not authority but reason, not cynicism but faith in man, faith in God. Our strength lies in the fearless and untiring pursuit of truth by the minds of men who are free. This I do believe.

What as individuals, can we do to safeguard and to nourish this great inheritance? I say: Search our minds and our souls and find out what it is we believe about democracy and about America. Knowing that, hold fast to that in which we believe, and let neither force from without, nor guile nor fears from within, cause us to forsake those precepts in which as Americans we deeply believe, and from whence comes our strength.

1 . FREEDOM AND FEAR

Freedom and Fear

W HAT is it we in America have to fear? And what action can we take to minimize cause for fear?

We do have cause to believe that we may someday be the target of military aggression. That is clear enough. To brood over this potential hazard, however, to wallow in the horrible details (as some speakers and writers do) can do no good; since it prods fear almost to the brink of panic, it is definitely harmful to our strength. As prudent and realistic people we know this danger of war is not a fanciful one. We have, therefore, set out to do something about it by the building, at vast cost, of the greatest peacetime military power in our history, and the greatest anywhere in the world today. We are developing atomic weapons; we have able and devoted military leadership; the country is not apathetic, nor misled, nor divided on this issue.

Nor do we base all our hopes of preventing armed aggression on military force alone. Our program of economic aid to other countries, in support of our foreign policy and in the interest of peace, is the most comprehensive in history. The prospects of international order and law, through the step-by-step strengthening of the United Nations and its related agencies to develop a solid basis of international community, is one of the most impressive efforts in the long quest for peace.

There are fears of an American Fifth Column, of widespread disloyalty among our own people. Indeed there are those among us who are completely preoccupied with dealing with this hazard, almost to the exclusion of everything else that can be done to protect and foster democracy. That we are in such a state of internal danger seems to most people, I think, an exaggerated and extreme view. The authorities charged with enforcing the laws against disloyal and subversive acts would be better able to carry their responsibilities if those noisy individuals for whom the general public has such low esteem did not so often make this potential danger their chief personal stock in trade.

On the whole, it seems to me, we are dealing with the problem of infiltration in an active and a sensible way. The wise course here is that we be neither naive (which we certainly have not been) nor given to panic, of which there have likewise been only sporadic signs.

Still another fear is the fear of depression and economic insecurity. But have we ever been better prepared to prevent a grave depression; have we ever been as experienced in the use of government powers to stimulate and strengthen private economic activity? It seems clear to me that there is but little basis for any profound fears that we shall fall victim of a prostrating period of unemployment and economic chaos.

It is not, I believe, fears of armed agression, or the sudden overthrow of our democracy by disloyal Americans, or of economic depression that chiefly account for the concern and worry about the future among a growing segment of thoughtful Americans. Our disturbed state of mind goes to something more fundamental, more subtle and more immediate.

Our fears, I think, can be said to center about this question: "How can this people, now the sword and the shield of freedom in the world, best protect democracy and individualism against the menace that is embodied not so much in the threat of Communist force and violence as in Communist ideas, practices and philosophy of life?"

We are perplexed and fearful, I believe, chiefly for these two reasons. First, because we see almost daily evidence that in the very steps we take to defeat communism we may imitate that very regimentation of thinking, and that very domination of private affairs by politicians and political methods against which we have set out to fight. We are fearful when (in the very first years of what will be a long contest) we observe here at home a tendency toward the enforcing of orthodoxy of thought and toward increasing governmental inspection of opinions and of private lives.

Second (and a corollary of the first), although there is no substantial pro-Communist sentiment in this country, we are not dead sure how firmly committed many of our own people are to democratic moral and ethical precepts, nor how well, in a contest with Communist cynicism, we will live up to our belief in open and fair dealing and concern for the individual. In the world scene we are in a sense the country boy on his first trip to the big city. How

well will we fare when our democratic ideals and sense of
decency and our devotion to the dream of individual
freedom are exposed to an ugly, "worldly-wise" contempt
for those idealistic values? Will we hold on to our faith in
that contest?

On this score we are especially uneasy and concerned
about our young people. With their natural and wholesome curiosity and their inexperience, dare we take the
risk of permitting them to be exposed to Communist
ideas? Is not the risk too great that they will not have
enough discrimination to see the contrast between the
idealistic words with which communism is sometimes
clothed, and the actual practice which is so complete a
denial of idealism?

These I think are the basis of our most deep-seated wor-
ries and fears today. These fears, even those that appear
on the surface to deal with our American concerns alone,
are actually closely related to the great contest with communism. The mortal rivalry that suddenly engulfs us
touches and affects almost every aspect of our life. It
forces us to re-examine and look anew at practices and institutions we had always regarded as exclusively our own
concern—"nobody else's business" we used to say. The
weak, or even ugly spots in American life (that is, weak
measured by our own ideals and standards), now take on
a changed significance.

The most obvious illustration, of course, is a serious
economic illness, such as large-scale unemployment. We
know a prolonged depression would be exploited to the
utmost by communism throughout the rest of the world

(as well as within this country) as evidence of the failure of American democracy. Most people therefore realize that a depression—and the suitability of countermeasures —have overnight ceased to be merely a matter of our internal economy. Another example: the fairness or unfairness with which Negroes accused of crime are dealt with has taken on an international significance, as has the provision for Negro education and economic opportunity. Similarly, there is hardly an incident of blatantly irresponsible journalism, or of public corruption or private greed that is not grist to the mills of those who are trying to break down the position of this country as the standard-bearer for the democratic way of life.

America's sudden coming to unmistakable world preeminence no less than the fury of the Communist attack compels us to re-examine in the light of our new role in the world, many of our ideas and institutions, among them some we had generally supposed were settled.

Our views about our military establishment provide one illustration. Our fixed democratic idea about a military organization has always been that it should be inconsequential in size, in cost, and in its influence upon our normal civilian concerns except in a time of clear emergency. Then—and usually at the last moment—we give it everything we've got, build it up swiftly and disband it just as swiftly.

Because this has been our fundamental policy we have never had to concern ourselves about the dangers of military domination or undue influence upon American government, business, education, and social standards.

Other nations, as recent history bears witness, have had a different habit about the place of the military, and have had quite different results than ours. But now as an immediate consequence of the abrupt change in our role in the world, this traditional policy has been reversed. We have today a large and costly military establishment, and the chance that for twenty-five years at least it will ever be less than a major factor in our daily lives and civil institutions seems to me quite remote. For years to come it will have an effect on private industry as the largest buyer of industrial products; an influence in education, as a principal source of funds for scientific research and development; a profound influence upon the tax structure, and upon public expenditures since it is one of the largest claimants for tax receipts; and generally a very direct factor in the day-in and day-out affairs of civil government and hence of the political life of the country.

Such are a few among the many changes in America. We do not make such changes from our traditions gladly; quite the reverse. They are regarded as the necessary consequences of a change in the world which we did not seek, in fact sought to avoid. But these great changes should not and need not be a cause of fear.

Communism's strong reliance upon fear is logical, just as democracy's reliance upon faith is consistent with its underlying thesis. Even a casual examination of fear and its consequences make this plain.

Fear spawns ugly children, such offspring as envy and hatred of those more fortunate or more secure. Fear and envy encourage preoccupation with self in which it is each man for his own hide and the devil take his neighbor. Men caught by fear turn to repression. When men deliver themselves to their fears they are not likely to listen to leaders who are bold, creative and noble; they tend to hearken to little men, men who are by nature defensive and negative. Deep fear shakes men so that they seek the absolute answers of authority, not of reason.

What is it about communism's ideas and philosophy and practices that we want most to keep out of our own lives?

Communism has demonstrated that it is built upon a profound distrust of the individual human being. Hence its insistence upon "official" thinking, upon uniformity of thought and even of artistic taste, and upon the use of secrecy and informers and force to exact that uniformity. Such repression of independent individual action, thought, and taste has the effect of replacing authority for reason, and of substituting force for a faith in the potentialities of the human spirit. These are among the precepts we are so strongly opposing.

It is helpful, in learning how to fight off such ideas, and the systems of tyranny by which they are enforced, to take a look at how repression actually works in the field of science, in contemporary Russia.

In Russia, domination of science and technology by politicians and their ideas and fears is virtually complete. It covers more than science, however: politicians rule the minds of the writers and publishers of books and newspapers, the producers of motion pictures, even those who compose music and write poetry, as well as those who are teachers.

The theme of the official Russian science seems to be that an idea that originated in the mind of a non-Russian and a non-believer in communism is *scientifically* wrong.

Nuclear physics is one of the most recent fields to feel the effect of orthodoxy. There is, for example, the case of a prominent atomic scientist, whose story one finds in the Russian publication *Literary Gazette* for November 20, 1948, Associate Academician Y. I. Frenkel, Stalin prize winner in 1947, member of the Leningrad Physical and Technical Institute. He is now in disgrace because Russian officials found that he favored a theory of the atom and the electron that happens to be well accepted among the scientists of America and other Western democratic countries. That, however, was not the whole of his crime. His inquisitors discovered that this Russian scientist was a member of the *American* Physical Society and the National Geographic Society of the *United States*. This "guilt by association" apparently helped demonstrate to his political superiors his lack of scientific qualifications.

In the field of biology, too, un-Russian ideas have been banned by the politicians. In genetics, Russian scientists have now been told what side their chromosomes are buttered on. A recent case is that of a geneticist, A. R. Zhedrak. He had disputed the view that acquired characteristics can be inherited, views espoused by Lysenko and Michurin—two other Russian geneticists. While a spirited argument about who was right was in progress among geneticists, Zhedrak found that the politicians

had decided the dispute, and against his contention. So
he was not only scientifically wrong—by definition—but
his loyalty to his country was now in doubt.

He had to recant in a passage that is tragic and humil-
iating and medieval. "So long as our Party," he wrote,
"recognized both tendencies in Soviet genetics, and disputes between those tendencies were viewed as creative
discussions in contemporary science, thereby assisting in
the discovery of the truth, I steadfastly defended my
views, which in part differed from the views of Academician Lysenko. Now that it has become clear to me
that the basic postulates of the Michurin tendency in
Soviet genetics have been approved by the Central Committee of the Communist Party, I, as a member of the
Party do not consider it possible for me to retain a position that has been recognized as erroneous by the Central
Committee of our Party."

Russian education is in much the same state of affairs.
Political orthodoxy, and schooling in Communist economic dogma and not the pursuit of truth, are the major
concerns of Russian schools and teachers. In a recent
article a Soviet educator states "the Soviet schools cannot
be satisfied to rear merely educated persons, but should
instill the ideology of Communism in the minds of the
young generation, shape a Marxist-Leninist world out-
look and inculcate the spirit of Soviet patriotism and
Bolshevik ideas." The direction of Soviet teaching, and
education in general, is not in the hands of professional
educators or school officials, or teachers, but of the
politicians and the bureaucracy.

My present responsibilities as a public servant bring me in daily touch with science and technology; this opportunity to observe the ways of science makes it clear that it flourishes best in an atmosphere in which individual freedom of thought and inquiry are encouraged and stimulated.

The democracies excel, and I believe shall continue to excel in science and technology, because they are the special province of individualism. They depend upon ideas, upon independent and sometimes unconventional or unpopular kinds of thinking by individuals. The direction and control and policing of thought and inquiry and education at the hands of political or economic leaders will wither and kill the progress of science and technology.

It is not, however, so much what we are *against* as what we are *for* that causes us to oppose communism. We believe in the human spirit. We believe in reason and the inquiring mind. We believe in the moral law and the supremacy of God.

Our course should be continually to examine into our fears, for they are not without foundation. We need to do this with as great detachment as we can; but we must continually be on our guard.

But it is not our fears nor our defensive measures that will bring the ultimate victory. The chief danger is not that communism itself will take us over. The danger is that in the strain of the contest against Communist ideas and defensive efforts to prevent its growth we shall aban-

don the very attributes of democracy that give us strength
at home and moral leadership abroad.

We cannot, for example, successfully oppose communism by political governmental directions as to what
shall and shall not be taught in our schools and universities. By the measures necessary to police such suppression
of any ideas with which we disagree, or to search out the
relatively few disloyal teachers, we risk the weakening of
our whole democratic structure. We cannot successfully
oppose communism by setting out to create and to utilize
an opinion-police; but we can thereby corrode the very
democratic strengths we seek to preserve.

A democracy can best defend itself by living in its faith,
by remaining a democracy. A democracy can best survive
and prosper when its people understand ever more clearly
wherein lies its strength, what it is fighting for and why;
by recognizing upon what a noble foundation democratic
life stands: the finest expression yet attained of an ancient
aspiration of man, that to be worthy of his Creator he
must be free.

2. THE WELLSPRINGS OF OUR VITALITY ARE ETHICAL AND SPIRITUAL

The Wellsprings of Our
Vitality Are Ethical
and Spiritual

THE anxious peoples of the world are bedeviled and often confused by many voices in their own lands, telling them just what America is like, what our motives are. The confusion abroad is natural enough. We should take care, however, that we ourselves do not get confused about the sources of our strength, nor about what it is that makes America strong and that will keep her strong.

What is this source and this foundation of our American strength? The answer most commonly heard is: our economic system. This "system" is variously referred to as the capitalist system, or democratic capitalism, or the system of free enterprise, or some similar expression.

The central role of free, competitive, private enterprise in the life of America can hardly be exaggerated, but neither this nor any other answer in economic terms alone can explain our basic vitality.

The basic source of the strength of American democracy does not lie in an "economic system." The wellsprings of our vitality are not economic. They go deeper still: they are ethical and spiritual. Our society in Amer-

17

ica is founded not upon the cold and bloodless "economic man" of the Marxist, but upon a faith in man as an end in himself.

We believe in man. We believe in men not merely as production units, but as the children of God. We believe that the purpose of our society is not primarily to assure the "safety of the State" but to safeguard human dignity and the freedom of the individual. As a people we have built upon a faith in the spirit of man. We conceive that the development and happiness of the individual is the purpose and goal of American life. We are not ready to "trade in" this luminous concept of a people's purpose for the notion that the America of the Bill of Rights, of Walt Whitman and Justice Holmes and Abraham Lincoln, is simply a highly productive economic system.

What we have, actually, is not a system at all, but almost its opposite. Ours is a society of the greatest imaginable diversity and flexibility. We take things as they come, deciding how to handle situations by the facts of each situation itself—"doing what comes naturally." The only way in which it can be said to be a "system" is to say that our "system" is to have no system.

The vitality of our distinctive institutions of production and distribution of goods ultimately depends not upon rigid and fixed economic principles but upon ethical and moral assumptions and purposes. Our unparalleled productivity and standard of living are not the consequence of an economic system, but rather the other way around. Our economic success and our flourishing economic institutions are the consequence of our ethical and

moral standards and precepts, and of our democratic faith in man.

In America we have ethical guide lines. We have developed rather highly a sense of what is right and what is wrong, what is fair and decent, and what is just crude use of arbitrary power. We can be fooled for a time by a cynical labor leader or business giant, by a politician or public official who conceives of American society as nothing more than a jungle in which the most ruthless prevails. Sometimes we are slow to repudiate disregard of our democratic faith. That faith is always there, however, as the foundation of our buying and selling, our hiring and firing, our political and financial institutions. No factory can be operated, not a carload of wheat sold, not a labor dispute mediated, not an election held, that these ethical, legally unenforceable precepts are not part of the transaction.

I do not see how our kind of society could flourish in any other way. This is a highly interdependent country. It is therefore too complex for rigid planning or for the legal enforcement of detailed plans. If we are to function at all, it must be in a relatively loose, informal way. The sanctions we impose must of necessity be largely ethical and moral, based less upon law than upon commonly accepted standards of fair play and respect for human integrity. This is the way we do function, by and large. This is the reason we flourish.

There are those who would not agree with me in this analysis. They would have us believe that we are free and strong because we excel in making millions of the same kind of useful gadgets. That seems to me to have the cart before the horse. I assert that it is because freedom for men is a primary ethical concern of ours that we do so well in making gadgets and raising food and doing successfully many other things—among them the winning of wars.

Diversity and flexibility rather than a stereotyped hard and fast system is an essential part of such a noble concept of society as ours. We get our economic services in the way that at the time seems to work best, that will in a particular situation best advance our underlying purposes. We do not start with all the economic or political answers. We make the answers up as we go along. Thus, American industry is owned and operated, by and large, by competitive private enterprise; yet in 1946 the Senate of the United States voted without dissent to establish public ownership and management in one of our largest industries, the atomic materials industry, and made it a government monopoly. That appeared to be the thing to do at the time, for reasons related to the facts of atomic energy, not for reasons taken out of some book of economic dogma.

The most rock-ribbed Midwestern town I know has for many years owned and operated its own electric power and light plant. Is this then a "socialist" town? Hardly! Its water service has been privately owned for the same period. There is a privately owned university; a public junior college. No one considers that these things are inconsistent; and of course they are not, except to the dogmatist who insists upon a fixed "system." In the same town there is a farmers' feed cooperative that is not quite private or quite public, operating side by side with a big privately owned feed company. There are private banks, there is a mutual nonprofit insurance company, there are state-owned liquor stores. We would never consider adopting government ownership or control of newspapers, partly because of their educational character; but our school system, the cornerstone of American education, is almost entirely publicly owned and managed. This is all part of the familiar picture of American diversity, of American flexibility.

The fact is that we have hardly an ounce of economic dogmatism in us. This diversity is a prime characteristic of ours. We have a great capacity to adapt ourselves to any need. All this stands us—and the world—in good stead these days. For among the nations of Western Europe there are many different kinds of economic undertakings and methods of control; and as befits world leaders we are peculiarly equipped by reason of our own economic diversity to deal effectively with each of these, without imposing our "system" on them or sacrificing our own unifying sense of purpose and direction, which is to advance the individual.

No honest person would deny that there are today some disturbing tendencies in our country away from our fundamental concern for the individual, away from our standards of fairness between men. We are witnessing in some quarters as ugly a scene of hoggishness and money-mania as we have seen since the days of the twenties. Many of those who spent the years of their youth fighting for this country returned to find themselves the victims of legal crookedness and outrageous speculation. These and many other evidences of disregard for our ethical precepts do exist in some quarters; and to the extent that they exist they poison the wells of our material as well as our spiritual strength.

We ourselves should be very clear about American fundamentals, as we move into the most fateful role we have ever played in world affairs. Our leadership in large part depends upon our continued capacity to demonstrate how superior our way of living is in human terms. It is important that we be clear in our own minds about the true sources of our strength; that we nourish and safeguard the ethical principles that make us strong.

3. MATERIAL PROGRESS *PLUS* FREEDOM

Material Progress Plus Freedom

TODAY the world is torn in a struggle between two opposing ways of looking at life. We are witnessing a clash between two quite different ideas of how governments can help to satisfy the desires of their citizens. This is the essential conflict.

The basic desires of men are much the same the world over. The average man seeks some security against want, ill-health, and old age. The problems of holding a job, of making a better living, or providing food and clothing and education for the family are the immediate ones that men and women everywhere face every morning and evening of their lives.

Unless we here in America continue to find solid answers to these economic problems faced by the average man we may find that tomorrow, without the aid of guns or atomic bombs, the rival way of life has won and our democratic system has perished from the earth.

The democratic system we believe in will be secure only if it serves its citizens effectively. The people have a right to expect an opportunity to share in the benefits of advances in science and research. They have a right to demand protection from economic abuses beyond their own individual power to control. They have the further right to insist that the methods of administration used to carry out the very laws enacted for their individual welfare shall not atrophy their human resources. They must not pay for a rising standard of living with the sacrifice of their civil and economic liberties to the demands of a remote and overcentralized government over which they can exercise little or no control. They must not be forced to yield their economic destiny to a concentration of powerful business groups.

We are not agreed in this country as to how we can achieve a higher standard of living for all and still remain free. But candid men of every political faith are clear that this is our major problem. We are divided on how to go about steadily and rapidly increasing our production and distribution. To the authoritarian mind it is a sign of weakness in the democratic capitalist system that we have no formula, no dogma which may not be disputed or questioned. The dictator nations are confident that in our lack of a disciplined system lies the advantage of their system over ours.

There are some in this country who believe that only the adoption of a system of communism or fascism will meet the needs of our time. On the other extreme, there is a larger and much more influential group, with another and equally dogmatic solution, who insist that private business alone can effectively raise our standard of living. They tell us that "private business must be free," unrestrained by governmental action taken in the interest of the rest of the community; that everything a public body undertakes is parasitical and unproductive.

Most of us in America today believe neither of these extreme doctrines. We repudiate any system which would deny us the right freely to dispute the validity of any political or economic dogma. Our democratic ideal is the active, thoughtful participation of as many people as possible in the public discussion that precedes decisions that vitally affect us as individuals, and the active joining of the people themselves in the affairs of their economic and political self-government.

It is true that such a conception makes at times for delays. This much must be conceded to the advocates of the rival system. Blind obedience guarantees quick decision and speedy action. Violence and terror will effectively smother discussion or dissent. But in the longer view, I believe democracy will triumph because its concern for its individual citizens, its respect for their dignity and judgment, will nourish a spirit that will be indomitable in the face of adversity.

We are coming to realize that the true measure of our strength as a nation is not our military establishment alone, but the vigor and health and, above all, the spirit of the people themselves, of the men and women and children on farms, in places of business, in factories, in banks, in railroad switchyards, in all the manifold activities that make up the living tissue of American democratic life. The struggle for American freedom will, I believe, be lost or won in the communities and in the homes of America. That country in which community life and home life have decayed, have grown weak and cynical, is a country which does not care enough for its freedom to be capable of retaining it.

We are coming to see that a free democracy cannot be successfully preserved unless the people as a whole regard it as more than just a phrase to be repeated in Fourth of July orations. Democracy is something that must be experienced and practiced in everyday life. It is quite literally a way of life—a way of *everyday* life.

As Americans, we cling to the Jeffersonian principle of the right of the people to choose the kind of community and industrial life which to them seems good. Jane Addams put it beautifully when she spoke of the two essentials of government, "truth and the consent of the people." This right of the people to choose necessarily calls for an informed leadership; but that leadership must be one that believes in men and women and their infinite potentialities, not a leadership which distrusts or patronizes the average man and woman.

This fundamental right to choose, moreover, cannot be an empty right. The people must be able to exercise a genuine option. They must be in an economic and political position in which they can exercise a free choice as to the kind of life they want to live.

Neither government nor business can guarantee prosperity. This is true for individuals and for regions. There is however much that the people themselves can do in a democracy to widen the opportunity for such prosperity and progress, for individuals, communities, and regions.

Everything depends upon *how* this action to widen opportunity and stimulate economic development is taken.

Everything depends upon the spirit in which that task is undertaken; upon its purpose, whether for the welfare of the many or the few; upon the methods chosen that will determine whether men will live in freedom and peace, or fear or terror; whether their natural resources will be speedily exhausted or will be made solid beneath their feet for themselves and for the generations to come.

Science and technology are tools for such widening of economic opportunity. The physical achievements that science and technology now make readily possible, however, may bring no benefits. They may indeed bring evil, unless they are conceived and carried out for the benefit of the people themselves. Without such a purpose, advances in technology and the industrialization of a raw material area may bring to the average man only a new kind of slavery and the destruction of democratic institutions.

The TVA is now known through the world as an example of American democracy in action. Here is an instance of democracy so organized as best to aid in the development of the natural resources of a region for the benefit of all of its people, but with their consent, their approval, and—most important—with their participation.

The Tennessee Valley is one of many evidences of the great vigor and vitality of modern democracy. All the vast engineering and industrial achievements that have taken place in the Tennessee Valley—a region of millions of people and an area as large as Great Britain—have been accomplished without the loss of a single liberty of the people.

The TVA organization is one of free men and women, free in every sense. They are, for example, free of political domination. They are not appointed to their jobs because of their political beliefs; in fact, the TVA law provides that if such a thing is done the directors shall be removed by the President. Men of all parties, races, and creeds have worked together. Those who work on this undertaking are not seeking to promote the power or the glory of any man or any small group of men. On the construction and operating jobs the wages and working conditions are agreed upon in contracts written at the conference table by the TVA management and organized labor, through honest collective bargaining. In the restoration of the fertility of the land farmers through their own community organizations have taken the leading part and make the important decisions themselves about the land on which they live. In each of the scores of communities of the Valley electricity is distributed by a board chosen by and wholly responsible to the local citizenry who own the electric facilities. I could mention many other illustrations to show that far-reaching as are the developments in this Valley they have not been the result of force and fear, but of consent and participation. The speed and efficiency and discipline that have marked this development have not been brought about by the knotted whips of any secret police, nor by the roar of an overpowering propaganda machine. One of the most extensive engineering and development accomplishments of modern times is a product of democratic methods and of men devoted to the principles of freedom.

Such facts as these mean much to all of us in these days. Totalitarians and ultrareactionaries insist that only by surrendering freedom may the physical needs of men be satisfied. They assert that only by the compulsion of fear and force is it possible to secure efficiency and good organization. Americans can point to the TVA as one of many concrete sets of proof to the contrary.

A project that has as its end the well-being of men and women and children and of providing for them the benefits of Nature's gifts, at the same time inspires the faith and the devotion that make men ready not only to work for their country but ready once more, if need be, to sacrifice all they have for its defense.

In the years to come we must prove by our achievements that in the United States of America we have the intelligence and the high courage to build a civilization so strong, so humane, so devoted to the welfare of the individual that it will survive whatever may transpire in other parts of the world. This is a magnificent task.

4. WANTED: NEW PATTERNS OF COOPERATIVE EFFORT

Wanted: New Patterns of Cooperative Effort

WE AMERICANS understand with great clarity that learning the art of getting along together is mankind's most difficult and by all odds its most important and most rewarding task. That great invention for getting along together we call the Constitution and Bill of Rights is mightier in our esteem than the invention of the electric dynamo. The fact that in Greater New York eight million people have developed ways of working together in peace and dignity is more important than all of New York's skyscrapers, world famous though they are.

One of the most beautiful phrases in our language are the words an American uses when he says to those with whom he has been in disagreement: "I'll go along with you. That's not the way I see it, but I'll go along." Out of this precept of reasonableness and respect for the opinions of others often issues one of the finest fruits of thought: a composite judgment, the product of many minds.

The considered judgment of men who reason together embodies more than "tolerance" which is, after all, a somewhat thin and negative concept. It is rather based on

35

an affirmative belief in the value of blending diverse experiences, diverse backgrounds. Such a composite or group judgment can be sturdier than any one of the individual or separate judgments that makes it up. This harmonizing of conflicting views into a common conclusion is not merely the trader's "splitting the difference"; it is not compromise for its own sake. It is a doctrine in exact contradition to the growing fanaticism and dogmatism in the world, in which differences from an official party line are dealt with as traitorous and in which the accommodation of conflicting ideas is regarded as a sign of weakness rather than what it is in fact: a mark of strength.

This respect for the other fellow's way of looking at things is characteristic of American life and, unhappily, not at all characteristic of present day life in many nations of Europe and Asia. In this country we encourage diversity of thought to such an extent that no man can truthfully assert that he speaks for all of any group of America's citizens.

We are all familiar with social inventions. These are devices men have painfully worked out to enable them to live together more harmoniously. Some are simple; a zoning ordinance, for example, or a traffic signal. Others are more complicated or more profound, such as a Bill of Rights and a Supreme Court that protect the liberties of the individual even against the action of a majority. Still another is the idea (at one time quite novel) of the whole community joining to hire men to carry pistols so every man need not carry one—the idea of a professional police force.

The idea of a United Nations organization is, of course, a social or human relations invention, on a world-wide scale. It is a great effort to develop among all peoples those very skills of living together in peace and justice and in generosity of spirit that we in this country have carried forward, among ourselves, with such heartening success.

Each of these social inventions, from the simplest to the most profound, was designed so that men might get along together with a greater measure of security, dignity, and opportunity. Such measures as these do not just happen, any more than atomic energy or radar, or a B-36 just happened. They are the product of thinking and of experiment. They are the product of many inquiring minds. These social inventions call for that openness of mind, high intelligence, and spirit of experimentation which are required for great scientific discoveries.

The day of science and technology in which we live increases rather than diminishes the importance of these social inventions. Learning how to make scientific advances serve mankind, and how to make them part of the stream of man's everyday living, is even more difficult and more subtle, and clearly more important than the solution of technical riddles. Physical discoveries can be made by a few men, or even one man (penicillin is an example) and thereafter their acceptance and use can come overnight. But social invention, new ways of getting along together, if they are to be effective, must be understood by people generally, and be acceptable to them. This is clearly true in a democracy. I am inclined to think that it is also true in any form of society.

The most noteworthy recent achievement of science and industry, the large-scale release of the energy within the nucleus of the atom, is a grand and dramatic illustration of this very proposition.

This development had behind it more than thirty years of the work of many minds in many lands throughout the world. The actual production of the atomic bomb itself came about because of the combined and cooperative efforts of men of science of Great Britain and Canada, as well as the United States.

Even before Pearl Harbor scientific knowledge useful in war was pooled between the United States and Great Britain. It was under that general policy that research on the atomic bomb began. In order to bring about production of atomic weapons as rapidly and as securely as possible, President Roosevelt and Prime Minister Churchill decided to locate and carry on the major portion of the actual work within the United States and Canada. A distinguished mission of British scientists came to this country and their work, especially at the Los Alamos, New Mexico, laboratory, contributed in an important and direct way to the success of the atomic bomb project. At Chalk River in Ontario there is today in operation a heavy water atomic reactor, the only one of its design, that is further tangible evidence of British-Canadian-American joint effort.

When the atomic bomb burst upon the world the three

governments recognized that this new and devastating force placed upon them and the rest of the world a grave responsibility. This feeling was expressed in the Truman-Attlee-King Declaration of November 15, 1945, which stated that the application of recent scientific discoveries requires that the entire civilized world devise means to insure that atomic energy shall be used for the benefit of mankind instead of a means of destruction. The three nations, again acting together, made the specific recommendation that the United Nations should establish a Commission to consider at once the problem of international control of atomic energy.

The wartime experience shared as partners in a joint venture by the three governments provides a demonstration of benefits to be derived from cooperative effort. The war over, the three governments concerned are continuing to recognize the benefits of joint effort. In January of 1948 they entered into an agreement for continued interchange of "scientific and technical information in certain defined areas, and collaboration on matters of raw material supply of common concern." Consequently, on many occasions scientists and technical men of two or of all three nations have met to consult and exchange ideas and experience on specific topics in more than a half dozen fields concerning atomic energy.

These arrangements of January 1948, however, are limited both in their scope and their duration; on July 29, 1949 President Truman announced the intention of the United States to explore with the United Kingdom and Canada basic questions underlying long-range co-

operation in this field in which there have been so many
new developments in all three countries since the end of
the wartime joint effort.

The even more difficult and more important task of
living with the atom, the problem of effective international control, is also one that has seen the pooling of the
minds and purposes and efforts of men in many countries. It is an effort thus far not crowned with success.
Far from it. But it is one that will and can be solved only
by the principles of human cooperation, principles
espoused by the spokesmen of this country and of many
other nations, as they were discussed, for so many months,
within the Atomic Energy Commission of the United
Nations.

The American proposal for international development
and control of atomic energy, the Baruch plan, stands as
a significant event in man's moral history. That proposal
would have extended on a world-wide scale the cooperative principle so central to American democratic life, the
principle of cooperation among all men and among all
nations, applied to the development of atomic energy for
all of its vast benefits. The same measures of cooperation
would have extended to all mankind safeguards against
the misuse of atomic energy for destruction and coercion.

This proposal attempted to answer the question: How
can atomic energy be developed and controlled so that it
will be used only for the advancement of human welfare
and not be used for war and destruction? As a central part
of the search for a way to eliminate war this remains one
of the world's most vexing questions today.

In the attempted working out of an answer to this concrete and specific problem there is created an even broader opportunity for mankind. Its successful solution might contribute greatly to the prevention of war by removing one of its most fertile causes, a constant and ever-increasing fear of surprise attack by this new weapon which so lends itself to surprise use. It is difficult to see how the United Nations can fulfill its functions unless it makes real headway with this problem.

More affirmatively, the plan proposed first by this country can become an authentic though limited demonstration of world administration and the rule of world law. Though at first confined to one vital field, elimination of atomic weapons, it is only by collaboration among the nations and peoples of the world that this can be accomplished and the full benefits to men of this magnificent discovery realized.

The heart of the proposal, it seems to me, is not fear of catastrophe alone, nor detection of violators, nor punishment of wrongdoers. It is something more affirmative and hopeful: the establishment of a greater degree of community among the peoples of the world working together on undertakings of common and mutual benefit. It was the hope and the belief of those of us who laid the groundwork for this plan that out of the proposed world-wide Atomic Development Authority might come, as we said, "new patterns of cooperative effort . . . capable of extension to other fields." Indeed, we said we were "even sustained by the hope" that this program dealing with atomic warfare might contain seeds that in time could grow into that cooperation between peoples which may bring an end to all war.

We cannot have a world we want if we have atomic warfare. The two are contradictory. They cannot exist together. And since from now on it seems inevitable that before the end of any major war atomic weapons will be used, it is clear that we cannot have another such war if we are to have the world we want. We cannot wish ourselves out of this situation. Wanting a way out isn't enough; we must quite consciously and deliberately invent a way to control atomic energy and to channel it to useful and beneficent purposes.

We now have a job of social invention ahead of us, to match the invention of the scientists and technicians.

We build, in science and in social life and in international relations, upon what we have and what we are. But the edifice that is built upon this foundation must be one that looks out upon man as he wants to be, one that faces his future, not his past, one that satisfies the unconquerable aspiration of men and women to make tomorrow better than yesterday.

5 . SCIENCE, TECHNOLOGY
AND THE HUMAN SPIRIT

Science, Technology and the Human Spirit

THE revolutionary consequence of man's increased scientific, technical, and managerial talents is one of the central facts of our time. It touches the lives of all of us, wherever we live. It affects our health, our daily tasks in factory and farm and office, even our spiritual concepts. It profoundly affects our prospects for survival itself. For the release of atomic energy and the transmutations thereby of the very elements themselves—the supreme demonstration thus far of man's scientific talents —is knowledge that if used in a future war will bring catastrophic consequences. Yet used for peaceful purposes it is already bringing great blessings to mankind, with the clear promise of even greater benefits to come.

These are indeed magnificent new tools that our technology has fashioned. But those who believe in democracy have deep questions that we must ask, and that need to be satisfactorily answered before accepting technology as a genuine advance.

We want to know what are the consequences of technology for the human spirit. What is the relation of scientific advance to the inner life of man? How does it affect that mighty and precious intangible, man's sense of stewardship to God and to his fellow man? Can science and technical skills be used to further that inner life, to enrich and dignify human personality, to fortify the things of the spirit? These are urgent and vital questions. The answers are far from self-evident.

There is a relation between man's new vast power to change his environment and his inner life; this seems to me clear. The problems created by atomic energy and other dramatic evidences of man's increased physical powers are so new that he can hardly keep abreast of them. They give rise to spiritual perplexities that make his need for guidance more rather than less urgent. What these changes mean as they relate to man's responsibility to God, how they affect the soul of men, calls for the special training and the special insight of philosophers and of churchmen. But thoughtful laymen too perhaps may have much to contribute to the answering of these great questions, out of their experience and their deep concern.

My own experience has deeply persuaded me that centralization of administration in government and in business is a dehumanizing force. I am convinced that it is one of the chief causes in modern times of an erosion of the human spirit, an increase in the arbitrary and corrupting power of men over other men. Science and technology make this issue of centralization doubly critical, for scientific advance lends itself so readily to an increased concentration of power over the lives of others. As technology has been managed thus far it has, by and large, rather diminished than increased the average man's accountability for and participation in the vital decisions of his daily life. As a consequence of this trend men's ethical standards are threatened with atrophy, and a weakening of that respect for the sacredness of human personality without which the concept of man's steward-ship to God is rendered empty and meaningless.

The ultrareactionary and the ultraradical both assert that these losses of human values are the inevitable price of technical physical advance. This I deny. But I do not deny that the hazards to the human spirit exist. I know they are real. No one today can disassociate himself from the spiritual dangers that technology multiplies, nor from every effort to develop methods of administering technology that will magnify, not stultify, the spiritual worth of man. A man wants to feel that he is important. He wants to be able not only to express his opinion freely, but to know that it carries some weight; to know that there are some things that he decides, or has a part in de-ciding, and that he is a needed and useful part of some-thing far bigger than he is.

This hankering to be an individual is probably greater today than ever before. Huge factories, assembly lines, complex and seemingly mysterious mechanisms, and standardization in general all underline the smallness of the individual, because they are so fatally impersonal. If our intensive technical development could be made per-sonal to the lives of most men; if they could see themselves (because it was true) as actual participants in that de-velopment in their own communities, on their own land, at their own jobs and businesses—there would be an opportunity for a fortifying kind of individual satisfaction, and there would be stronger and happier men.

Here is democracy's great advantage in a technical world over communism and other forms of centralized and monolithic systems. It is the unique strength of genuinely democratic methods that they provide a way of stimulating and releasing the individual resourcefulness and inventiveness, the pride of workmanship, the creative genius of human beings whatever their station or function. A world of science and great machines is still a world of men; our modern task is more difficult, but the opportunity for democratic methods can be even greater than in the days of the ax and the hand loom.

A method of organizing modern technical development so that it draws in the average man and makes him a part of the great job of our time—in the day-to-day work in the fields and factories and laboratories and the offices of business—will tap riches of human talent that are beyond the reach of any highly centralized, dictatorial, and impersonal system of development based upon remote control in the hands of a business, a technical, or a political elite.

The spiritual yield of democratic methods, a renewed sense that the individual counts, would be justification enough. There is yet another reason, and a very practical one, for seeking at every turn to bring people actively into the task of building the technical foundation of modern society. It is simply this: There is really no other way in which the job can be well done. My experience in the Tennessee Valley seems to me to confirm this.

The whole world has sent some of its best minds to the Tennessee Valley to observe that undertaking. What they see is a systematic attempt to utilize the resources of nature and of technical knowledge in the service, not of science for its own sake, as a modern graven image, not of the State or of some new political or bureaucratic elite, but of individual human beings, *their* well-being, *their* hopes, and *their* purposes.

As the people of the Tennessee Valley believe, and as most observers agree, there is occurring in that Valley a change for the better in terms of opportunity for the individual in higher income and toward better living. The Tennessee Valley represents rather spectacular changes in a physical sense. A major river is changed into a chain of lakes that are controlled to serve men. Hillsides that once were eroded and infertile now are green and secure. There are electric pumps in farmyards, electric appliances in farmhouses. There are stronger local institutions, better schools, libraries, increased educational and recreational facilities. There are new factories, large and small. There are barges on the new river channel. These and many other changes make it a new Valley. The job of development is far from complete, of course. But it is well on the way. It is one more demonstration that modern technical and managerial skills and tools can change the physical setting of men's lives.

Equally impressive are the statistics of increased production of farm and factory, of rising individual income.

But this is not the real significance of what has transpired in the Valley of the Tennessee. What is really im-

portant is that there has been a change in the spirit
of the people themselves, a change in the direction of
greater self-confidence, as they have had more diverse out-
lets for initiative and enterprise in business, in farming,
in education, in civic affairs, and in the whole range of
living. This American experiment has fortified men's
confidence that human beings need not be chained to the
wheel of technology, but that man can use the machine
in the interest of human welfare.

The ultimate test of the improvement of man's environment is not a material one. It is embodied in the
question—and it is essentially a spiritual question—
What is happening to the inner quality of the human
beings affected by these material changes? Are they more
free than before? Do they feel more secure? Has the range
of their free choices been widened? Are they better able
to build their own happiness? Are they more disposed to
deal generously with their fellows?

In all our efforts to improve the lot of man through
technical development we must face a fundamental problem. That problem is to find ways, in promoting physical
well-being, to nourish and protect the integrity and the
promise of human personality.

This is at its base a moral issue, and the stuff of our
daily lives. Each day we must meet the test this issue presents—in business dealings, in legislative halls, in union
meetings. For in the application of science to men's lives
there is a perennial and unremitting conflict between
two opposing precepts that thread their way through
every phase of American life: on the one hand there is

faith in man's stewardship to God as the common Father of all of us; on the other, there is the conflicting concept of power, of the power of men over other human beings. Between these two opposing beliefs we see reenacted, under the fierce and sometimes terrible light of modern science and concentrated political power, the age-old struggle between those who would use men as a means of power and those to whom men are the children of God, and therefore not means but ends in themselves.

In this struggle which engages and deeply involves us all it is inspiring to observe our growing impulse to turn to one another for counsel and understanding: administrators, businessmen, farmers, workers, scientists, churchmen. It is perhaps a promise and a portent of that integration and wholeness that our fragmented and divided world so desperately needs.

6. A SENSE OF UNITY IN AN AGE OF SPECIALIZATION

A Sense of Unity in an Age of Specialization

THE passionate devotion to the dignity and supreme importance of human beings and the human spirit that underlies Christianity and Judaism is the mainspring of democracy. Here is a strong, clear central idea to unify the work of technicians and administrators, and of all men. That single idea has far more to be said for it, even from the narrowest utilitarian point of view, as a mark on the horizon and as a guide line for the direction of the energies of a technical society, than has the unifying idea of the totalitarians which is the glorification of material power and the force of the state.

At war or in peace, the modern world calls for highly specialized technical skills. To say today that a man is a chemist, or a mechanical engineer, or a forester is no longer enough; specialization has been carried so far that these classifications are now too general. This specialization of functions is reflected, of course, in our training in the universities and technical schools. We are threatened, as a consequence, by a measure of disunity and disintegration of our culture and underlying philosophy of life, for the quality of unity in thinking has been displaced by the philosophy of the specialist.

55

Modern technology is the product of specialization. In order to guide and control it, therefore, we must strive to revive the power of generalization, and thus to unify all of these highly specialized skills.

The striking thing I have found, as one responsible for over-all results, is that so frequently each of these highly specialized technical groups is fighting (sometimes politely, sometimes not politely at all) for the pre-eminence of his particular specialization, in a competition with some other. Whatever the professional specialization, too often I have found among technical men a clear, lively picture of one's own field and of its importance, and a dim and sometimes disdainful view of the other specializations.

A major problem of modern life is to forge the various technical skills together. This is not only urgent; it has proved to be very difficult to achieve. In my experience I have found that the more intense and imaginative the specialist is about his field, whether it be a narrow segment of soil chemistry, neutron diffraction, uranium metallurgy, fish life, statistical methods, and so on, the more likely he is to see everything else as just an adjunct to that specialized province of his. This results in disunity of thinking and hence confusion and disunity of the spirit.

The philosophical or spiritual consequences to an individual bereft of any sense of unity are likely to be disastrous. There is a sense of frustration. Any clear meaning to life vanishes. When that sense of frustration dominates a people men are likely to turn to war and the preparation for war, psychological and physical, to supply that meaning, for it sometimes happens that leaders and the man on the street alike come to prefer bloodshed and privation to a baffling vacuum.

Without the fusing and harmonizing of the separate and specialized forces that are part of modern life we may find increased governmental activity itself a confusing and disintegrating rather than a building force. Skillful coordination can add a surplus over and above the sum total of the same activities carried on without this intense concern for their relation one to another.

Sometimes you may add two and two and get zero. Technical research and development in the processing of farm raw materials without regard to the life of the soil from which the raw materials come may result in an exhaustion of the soil. That may mean the early death of the manufacturing operation which relies upon those farm raw materials. The desolate, abandoned sawmill towns of northern Wisconsin and Michigan, in the midst of cut-over forest land, are a bitter demonstration that sometimes when one adds an industrial operation and a great natural resource, the result may, if a sense of unity and relationship is absent, prove that two and two are zero. Two such activities as these—forestry and the processing of the forest's products—should and can be carried on so they will not cancel out each other, but with a sense of unity be made to add a plus value.

The two undertakings with which I am most familiar —TVA and atomic energy development—rest upon almost all modern technical skills. An administrator responsible for the end result must try to join these skills together according to some kind of generalization in his mind. TVA's experience offers a clue as to how we may overcome this disintegrating force that by a curious irony is itself the product of our great technical skill.

Although the administrators of the TVA have been given a kind of "power to decide," in broad terms and in accordance with the principle of unity of management, they do not seek to resolve conflicts among experts by the force of arbitrary decisions. Rather it is a common idea, an idea underlying the whole enterprise and common to every part of it, a democratic and essentially spiritual idea, that ties together and unifies the work of all the technicians, however highly specialized. The central "TVA idea" of the development, conservation, and use of the natural resources of a region for the benefit of its people has come to be the focus of the labors of all TVA technicians. Since the common idea is at once recognized as beyond the scope of accomplishment of any single specialization, a narrow competition between specialized techniques is discouraged; not the success of a single technique but of all is necessary.

An agency, public or private, whose sole responsibility, for example, is to supply electricity to farmers, might push as hard as possible for an increase in its corporate electric revenues regardless of how the farmer used the power he bought. The TVA has a business responsibility for dollar electric revenues. It has an equally great public responsibility for the well-being of a region. It is not therefore free to concentrate alone on building up dollar

revenues. The pressure on a farmer to pay the electric
bill for conveniences might mean less funds available to
him for the protection and increased fertility of his soil.
Accordingly, the TVA's emphasis in its electric promotion and its research and development of inventions
has been upon those uses of electricity which will increase
the over-all economic strength of the farmer and his
family.

Specialists from several fields have worked together to
achieve this end result. Quick-freeze units technically
designed especially for areas of small farm producers, for
example, open new opportunities for local, decentralized
industry. Even more significant is the effect of such a
technical development upon the conservation of the soil
and the income of farmers. Some of the crops, like peas,
are legumes that enrich the soil in which they grow. The
matted roots of strawberry plants help prevent erosion.
Frozen products cut down waste, bring rather high
prices, and tend to raise the farm income. As they get
more income from fewer acres, farmers keep the plow off
the steeper lands that wash badly and sow them to sod
crops. Here is a beneficent cycle under way: science and
engineering skill applied in a unified way to technical
problems of local industry that also helps the business of
farming.

Such a common objective gives a mark on the horizon
to each specialist that he knows is the same point at
which all the other specialists' attention is directed, or
should be directed. Out of this comes a relationship of
friendly harmony, so that specialists become co-workers

rather than annoying interferers in the ultimate "manifest destiny" of some specialized skill.

Technical efforts can be unified by an idea that is strong enough to draw them together. Democracy's concern for the individual is that unifying idea.

7. THE PURPOSE AND ATMOSPHERE OF SCIENCE AND TECHNOLOGY MUST BE MORAL

The Purpose and Atmosphere of Science and Technology Must Be Moral

SCIENCE is not simply a body of knowledge, it is a thing of the spirit. It is the spirit of adventure and the urge to know what lies beyond, the lure of new places, new knowledge, and new ideas. It is a way of thinking. It is the mind striving to be free of those prejudices which stand as barriers between ignorance and knowledge. It is a faith in the power of knowledge, a deep conviction that the truth can make men free. Above all science rests on a faith that man's hopes lie in expanding the area in which reason, not arbitrary force and power, directs his destiny and determines his relations to his fellow men the world over.

When one reflects upon the true nature of science, upon its spiritual aspect, one realizes why its progress depends so largely upon the freedom of inquiry and the interchange of ideas between free men. The creative powers of science stem directly from the ever-accelerating dissemination of information. The concrete results of scientific thought and scientific method that we see all about us have come about largely because there has been

the freest exchange of ideas among men capable of dealing in ideas. Scientific progress is actually measured (or
measureable) by the amount of scientific knowledge
abroad in the land.

Back of the dramatic discovery of atomic energy is a
long history of generation after generation of inquiring
minds, restless, questioning, testing, doubting, probing,
seeking the truth about the nature of the physical world,
about the procession of the seasons, about the sun in its
power and warmth, about the very stars in their courses.

Was this release of the basic energy of matter an event
over which we should rejoice, or should we tremble with
apprehension that man had at last let out of the bottle
an evil jinni too powerful to be tamed? We are not yet in
a position to judge of this question, for the time has been
far too short. We would not say today that the discovery
of fire is to be regretted. There is hardly a force more
beneficent in the life of man. When fire is out of control,
however, it can and does cause catastrophes of the most
horrible kind. We have learned to live with fire. Indeed
we can hardly imagine our civilization in its best aspects
without it. If, however, the only time we had ever seen
fire was in battle, pouring out of a flame thrower, con-
suming human life, or dropped from airplanes to burn
to a cinder a city of a million people, could we be sure
that it had been a good discovery?

Whatever answer the future holds, this much I believe
we must accept: There can be no putting the jinni back
into the bottle. To try to bury or to suppress new knowledge because we do not know how to prevent its use for

destructive or evil purposes is a pathetically futile gesture. It is, indeed, a symbolic return to the methods of the Middle Ages. It seeks to deny the innermost urge of the mind of man—the desire for knowledge.

Scientific research has become the right arm of modern technology, and to some people modern technology is plainly evil. They are homesick for a simpler life, before the days when man produced so much and knew so much. They want to flee. But where and how? They cannot say. They cry out against science and the machine and call them evil; but their voices are the voices of despair and defeat.

There are others who have an almost opposite view of the machine. We find them here in America, quite prominently in Russia, and indeed all over the world. What they say is exuberant and uncritical. "Of course technology is good—does it not produce more and more things, and is not production an end in itself?" They worship the machine. Efficiency is their god. The managerial elite are their high priests.

But suppose the spirit of man balks? Suppose the yearning to be human results in increased costs of production? Their answer is that man must be redesigned to fit the assembly line; it never occurs to them to revise the assembly line to fit man. The supertechnologists of the world are quite prepared to recreate man in the image of the machine.

The truth, however, would seem to be that the machine is neither good nor evil in itself. It is good only when man uses it for good. It is evil only if he puts it to evil purposes.

The machine can, of course, be so used as to degrade and enslave man. It can be used to exhaust the land and with it the dignity of human existence of those who live on the land; it can poison the air, foul the streams, devastate the forests, and thereby doom men and women and children to that spiritual degradation of great poverty which only great ascetics have been able to avoid. It can brutalize—and it has brutalized—men and women in factories and their children in the jungle of city slums. In warfare its horrors defy exaggeration.

The products of scientific research can do evil things, but it can also open wider the doors of human opportunity; it can nourish the spirit of men. Technology can be used to eliminate filth and congestion and disease; to strengthen the soil; to conserve the forests. In short it can humanize man's environment.

The engineers and skilled men who designed and built TVA's Fontana dam used technical knowledge to do it. That knowledge, built into that dam and into more than a score of others on the Tennessee River system, controls floods that in years past have caused great human suffering. Turbines and generators now produce electricity out of waters that once drowned men and destroyed their homes. That electricity travels over transmission lines to the huge plant at Oak Ridge, where it helps to make Uranium 235, the live material of atomic bombs. But electricity from the very same dams also goes down country roads to pump the water, saw the wood, and do much of the drudgery on many farms.

There is a similar duality in the product at Oak Ridge that this hydroelectricity helped produce. Uranium 235 is used in the most destructive weapon of all time; it is also the most intense package of stored power ever developed; some day the same material will produce power for farms and industries and hospitals.

We are not helpless. We can choose deliberately and consciously whether machines or human beings come first. But that choice will not be exercised on a single occasion, surrounded by spectacle and drama. We will move from decision to decision, from issue to issue, and all of us will be in the midst of this struggle for the rest of our days.

Great schemes of development are being proposed and planned for Africa and India and Siberia and Latin America and the Middle East. These and other underdeveloped areas of the globe are regions technology and science have hardly touched. Does it really matter what means are adopted to bring the fruits of science to the countless millions of physically wretched who live in these lands? Does it really matter that the purpose of such development may not be for human welfare? Will it matter if the people concerned do not have an opportunity to participate in the course of this development, do not have a voice in this new destiny that science and the machine can bring? Does it matter whether the purpose and the means are moral and ethical?

Nothing matters more profoundly.

We further the essential goodness of men by the simple act of faith in that goodness. And a lack of faith in the divine potentialities of the human spirit will of itself make men less worthy. These are the ultimate realities. It is by putting to practical use these realities that science and technology, by our deliberate choice, may be made to end hopeless poverty and widespread disease and bring in time a new era of fraternity among the peoples of the earth.

We cannot master the machine in the interest of the human spirit unless we have a faith in people. The rock upon which all these efforts rests must be a deep and abiding faith in human beings, an abiding faith in the supreme worth of life. It is not enough to provide more funds for physical research, more fine laboratories, more extensive projects in social research. It is not enough that there be more use of modern technology in this country or in South America or China. Even the most brilliant accomplishments of technicians and managers are not enough.

We cannot think of science and technology in the abstract, apart from the men who direct its course and its use, and who define the purposes for which it is put to use. To my way of thinking responsibility for the purpose and direction of technology may safely be entrusted only to those to whom the interests of human beings come first, who seek primarily to find what the people want and believe they need, not merely what those who control the research think they ought to want.

The purpose of technology and applied research

largely determines whether it is likely to further human well-being or threaten it. That purpose must be a moral one. Why? Because technology that is only "enormously developed intelligence" and leaves out the primary driving force in human affairs—the *spirit* of men—is bound to lead to one catastrophe after another, one war after another, each more horrible and mechanically perfect than its predecessor; to the exploitation and devastation of natural resources; and finally to the most terrible catastrophe of all, a nonmoral world.

Greater knowledge about the world will, I think, be the keynote of the immediate future. But greater knowledge alone will not be enough. There must also be greater love and understanding among men. And there must also be greater faith in humankind and in the purposes of the Creator of the Universe. Knowledge, love, faith—with these three the Atomic Age, the age in which we live, can become an age of mercy, of joy, and of hope, one of the blessed periods of all history.

8. BIG GOVERNMENT IS NOT INEVITABLE: AN ILLUSTRATION

Big Government Is Not Inevitable: An Illustration

DEMOCRACY, to be truly responsive to our aspirations for individual freedom, must increasingly develop and nourish and strengthen local institutions of government. Few precepts of American life are more deeply felt than this.

In actual practice, however, this policy has given way to a tendency that is its very opposite; an unbroken, and to me disquieting, increase in centralization of administration in Washington.

Here is a direct contradiction between the way we want our institutions of government to function, and the way in fact they do function. Some of those who bear responsibility for this weakening of democracy are unaware of the effect of what they are doing. Others, however, defenders or apologists for the trend, assert that centralized control by Congress and by the administrators in Washington cannot be avoided. Some public administrators and experts in government appear to be now in the process of seeking to persuade the American people that Big Government is inevitable.

I deny that Big Government is inevitable. I assert that there is a workable alternative, and that we should pursue that alternative to ever bigger Big Government. There is no wave of the future before which the American people and their great heritage of localized democracy are powerless.

To judge by what people say on this subject there is hardly anyone in private or public life who is in favor of what is taking place. And yet it goes right on, and at an accelerated pace. Surely this is a curious situation. Some of the most outspoken opponents of centralization I know (judging by their speeches) propose or support legislative controls or appropriation "riders" that make Washington control ever tighter. As a consequence one more prospect for genuine decentralization of Federal administration is dimmed or killed. By the same act they turn their back on still another opportunity to delegate to local, state, or Federal regional agencies functions that need not be and should not be administered by Washington bureaus nor controlled by the Federal Congress.

Federal aid to education provides an important illustration. There is almost universal *verbal* assent to the proposition that Federal financial support to education should avoid any trace of control from the Congress and the Federal departments in Washington.

But what has actually happened? The evidence is unmistakable that during the past twenty years (with support from both political parties), the trend has been in the other direction, and continues in that direction today.

The land grant college system, with its origin back in Lincoln's administration, provided the country a tested pattern whereby local and state institutions concerned with education could appropriately and productively receive Federal funds without the Congress and the Washington executive agencies sticking their fingers into education. Under one guise or another, however, the land grant college principle and practice has been steadily weakened. An opportunity for further decentralization in education has been lost. The new policy of Federal financial aid to the school systems of the states makes this recent history all the more a matter of practical and immediate concern.

Atomic energy development provides another illustration. The Atomic Energy Act of 1946 continued the Federal government as the proprietor of the most extensive scientific, educational, and industrial enterprise in all history. There is no alternative to Federal ownership, under present world conditions, for reasons I discuss in a later chapter. The Atomic Energy Commission recognized the dangers of excessive centralization in the Commission and remote control from Washington inherent in this nationalized enterprise, born of war. Since it was not possible nor desirable for the national government to divest itself of the ownership and over-all responsibility for the huge plants, laboratories, uranium refining operations, and research projects, a measure of decentralized administration appeared to the Commission as the best alternative that was open. That was the course followed. Extensive delegations, under broad contracts, were made from this Federal Commission to all manner of non-Federal institutions, including institutions of higher learning.

The Commission's program of research fellowships in basic science affords an illustration. The purpose was to help overcome promptly the acute and disturbing shortage of trained men in the fields of pure science. Following the principle of decentralization and to avoid Federal intervention in education, the actual selection of the research scholars to receive Federal stipends was turned over, under a contract, to the National Research Council of the National Academy of Sciences, outside the Federal government.

In a further effort to avoid excessive Washington office control the Commission set up regional operating offices throughout the country, in charge of Managers of Operations. The Managers are given broad authority and responsibility; they are not mere Chief Clerks, or paper shufflers, who must telephone Washington before making any decisions. (It is not well understood that decentralization is by no means synonymous with moving Federal officials out of Washington, into regional offices. If those field officials do not have a large measure of authority to make decisions, this is not decentralization at all, but only a rather expensive form of centralization.)

Such steps taken by the Atomic Energy Commission constitute a first step in the direction of avoiding the bane of Washington overcentralization.

The over-all results are encouraging. Entrusted with greater responsibility than under highly centralized Washington control, the industrial concerns and universities, engaged on work for the Commission, and the Managers of Operations have, in the main, shown initiative, have cut costs and improved processes, saving many millions of Federal dollars annually. Their incentive to continue to improve operations is increased by this method of dealing with them. On the other side of the ledger, mistakes have been made by the industrial and university contractors and by Managers, and inadequacies have developed, as would also be the case under a tightly controlled centralized form of operation.

The general trend toward centralization and Washington control, however, makes the Commission's effort to avoid the worst evils of Big Government in atomic energy quite difficult to sustain. Sentiment in Congress for tighter and tighter controls from Washington to be exercised by the Commission or Congressional Committees or the Bureau of the Budget tend to cancel efforts to encourage greater responsibility and initiative in the field, beyond the Washington scene.

Just what is the basis of the argument that Big Government is inevitable, and ever greater Washington control inescapable?

The stream of dialectics begins with a full agreement that "of course" everyone desires strong, dynamic local government in the communities and in the states of the United States. The Big Government apologists never question that proposition. We are told that these are "fine ideals"—the ideal of home rule, the ideal of a flourishing community and state government. Following close upon this disarming prelude, however, it is said that the complexities of modern living make this older ideal merely nostalgic. Our technical society, so they say, has made it obsolete and unworkable. The airplane, the telegraph, the telephone, swift transportation both within the United States and throughout the world make it regrettably necessary that the older ideal give way to the facts of modern life. Over and over again the story is repeated of the complex interrelation, the intricacies, the interdependence of American life. The nation has become a most complex fabric quite beyond the comprehension of the ordinary citizen, a fabric no longer separable, and hence national in its every aspect. What happens in Sacramento, California, affects a transaction in Portland, Maine, and so on. The thesis is too familiar to require repetition.

Generally speaking this is all true enough. But the conclusion that is drawn from this familiar picture is that since virtually every governmental problem has become a national problem, therefore every phase of government action must inevitably be administered nationally from Washington. Since—so the argument runs— local administration or state administration is obviously impossible where national interrelation is so complete, therefore Big Government is inevitable. We are told, in short, that Big Government is the price that must be paid for the wonderful technical development of this nation.

Those who have resigned themselves to this idea rarely defend centralization; they deplore it. They admit that remote administration from Washington is not desirable. They will even agree that the withdrawal of more and more decisions out of local communities and out of the state into Congress and into bureaus in Washington is unfortunate and corrodes our democratic institutions. They say however, that we must bow our heads before the inevitable trend toward centralization, because the nation has developed technically to such a point that centralized administration is the only means whereby a complex modern national economy can be governed. It is that or chaos. They assert that we must trust our legislators and administrators in Washington with more and more power of decision and control, with better and better tools of government. Why? Is it so that those in Washington may reverse this unwholesome trend, so they may decentralize and delegate to the agencies of the states and the communities? Not at all. It is so that these central government administrators may make centralization of administration more effective and efficient—more nearly uniform in its nationwide applications.

In any such discussion as this an important distinction has to be made. It is not new, but it is one that is often overlooked. It is the distinction between a national policy and central administration of that policy.

It is obvious that many problems that once could be dealt with as a matter of local or state policy now definitely require a national policy, determined through Congressional action. Problems once predominantly local in their scope and effect now have repercussions on other parts of the country—and the whole world for that matter—that did not exist in an earlier stage in our

development. These often require the enunciation of a
national policy and expenditure of Federal funds.

But because the central government through the
Congress must and should determine upon a national
policy in a particular field, it does not by any means
follow that *the administration of that policy* must necessarily also be on a nationwide basis. This distinction
between a centralized or national policy and the decentralized or localized administration of that national
policy, is a distinction of fundamental importance. It is,
moreover, a distinction the apologists of Big Government so frequently and persistently overlook. It is a
distinction which unless observed and respected by cor-
rective action in the way of decentralized administration
of national policies can lead to the progressive atrophy of
most local and state governmental functions.

The distinction between authority and its administration is a vital one. For a long time all of us—administrators, citizens, and legislators—have been none too clear
on this point. We have assumed that, as new powers were
granted to the government with its seat at Washington,
these powers therefore must also be administered from
Washington. We have taken it for granted that the price
of Federal action was a top-heavy, cumbersome administration. Clearly this is not true. The problem is to
divorce the two ideas of authority and administration of
authority.

Effective techniques of decentralization—not better
ways to centralize—should claim our first attention. The
very first question we should ask ourselves is: "Why can-

not these Federal activities be decentralized; if not in whole, why not in part?" The problem of first concern we must ever keep in mind is: Does this or that Federal program really have to be centralized and to what extent? Here is the real job to which our students and experts in public administration and our members of Congress should address themselves. It is a continuing, day-by-day task requiring the focus of administrative and legislative attention upon every opportunity for decentralization as it comes along.

The TVA is a concrete demonstration that ways and means can be devised to decentralize the administration of many of the functions of the central government. Indeed, one of the public's chief interests in TVA these days is as practical, living proof that despite the inter-relation of our vast country, despite the need for national policy on many matters heretofore local, the actual carrying out of those national policies can effectively be placed in the hands of local community and state agencies and instrumentalities. TVA's methods of decentralized administration may well prove to be the most important single product of the experiment in the Tennessee Valley.

The TVA, a public development corporation, is an agency of the central government. It was created by Congress. Its charter is a national charter. Its responsibilities and its powers derive from national powers defined in the Constitution of the United States. The responsibility of TVA, as defined by Congress, is to develop or aid the people of the Valley to develop and to utilize their natural resources in a region of substantial size, embracing parts of seven states of the Southeast. These functions and these responsibilites for natural resources and their development are in general, and taken one by one, familiar and long-time responsibilities and functions of the Federal government. They deal with navigation, flood control, electric power, the problems of our soils and forests, and research.

These are characteristic Federal functions. Nevertheless in virtually every aspect of the TVA's activities, TVA's management has found it possible to carry out such clearly Federal functions and policies through the medium of local community or state agencies and instrumentalities.

TVA is decentralized in more than one sense. First, it is a Federal corporation directed not from Washington but from the Tennessee Valley. It is not incorporated within any Washington bureau or department. This is the first step of its decentralization.

But there are other steps, made possible by the first, but of even greater importance. The TVA has by persistent effort delegated and thereby decentralized its functions so that most of them are carried out *not by Federal employees at all,* but by local and state personnel. This is effected by scores of contracts setting up joint partnership between TVA and cities, towns, counties, state boards of health, state conservation commissions, city power boards, farmers' cooperatives, county extension services, state agricultural colleges, state geology departments—the list could be continued to almost indefinite length.

As a consequence of this policy there are few functions of the TVA which could be executed by state or local agencies and personnel where that has not been the course chosen. The policies of TVA are national; the execution of policy is largely in local and state hands.·

During a period of American history when centralization of administration in Washington has increased at a rapid rate, in the Tennessee Valley state and local functions of government have grown, in diversity and strength, more rapidly than in any other region of the United States during the same period.

The record of TVA's more than sixteen years demonstrates that in the broad Federal field of development of natural resources—of river, land and farm, forests and minerals—there is a reasonable and workable alternative to centralized administration from Washington. The widespread approval of the TVA among the people of the Tennessee Valley region is attributed by the people themselves largely to this method of decentralization.

A few illustrations of TVA practice will make the point clearer. Agricultural development and control of water on the land, for example. The TVA has a responsibility in respect to the development of the land of the Tennessee Valley, as one of its basic natural resources. Part of that statutory responsibility arises out of the use Congress required TVA to make of the great laboratory and production plants at Muscle Shoals. These plants, built during World War I for munitions purposes (they again rendered service as munitions plants during World War II), TVA was directed to turn to the benefit of agricultural development in the Tennessee Valley, and elsewhere. This meant the manufacture of soil nutrients— chiefly the strategic soil mineral phosphate.

It was essential that there be made extensive practical tests and demonstrations of the value of new phosphate fertilizers being developed in those laboratories. Such testing, demonstration, and education on farms and among farmers was called for by TVA's Federal mandate.

To carry out this responsibility TVA did not set up a large central staff; it did not send Federal employees into the communities and onto the farms of the Tennessee Valley, which has become so common a practice in recent years. TVA rejected this method of further centralization and adopted a different course. We entered into a joint program (which was to be a *single* program) with the *state* colleges of agriculture, the *state* extension services, the *county* agent system. There is now almost fifteen years of experience under this arrangement to serve as a basis of judgment. The state extension services, the county agent system, and the state colleges of agriculture carry forward the actual demonstration and testing program, together with the agricultural education aspects involved, within the counties of the Tennessee Valley. Thus a Federal program, and state and local programs, became one. And it was and still is manned by and directed by the local agencies.

In this Federal activity of TVA the experts who deal with the farmers are not Federal employees. They are members of the staffs of the state colleges of agriculture and of the state and county extension systems. They are selected by those state and local agencies, not by TVA. The TVA, from its Federal appropriations, reimburses the local agencies for the salaries and expenses of these local experts who are carrying out a national policy and responsibility.

In a democracy, development of resources must ultimately rest upon the education of the people, the businessmen, the merchants, the farmers. This is not education in the narrowly defined schoolroom sense, but education which has as its purpose bringing facts and information to the people so that they may gain benefit from the best scientific knowledge, and do so without loss of diversity, local strength, and individual freedom. Providing funds by contract to the land grant colleges in the Valley states and for the county agent system of education and extension teaching seemed the best way to obtain these results in the agricultural program.

These institutions were local agencies adapted to an understanding of local diversities and needs, and subject to the control of the people locally. They combined facilities for teaching the young people, on whom progress in the Valley inevitably had to depend, with facilities for research and for extension. They were the recognized local agencies of agricultural education—not only in formal classes and in research, but through the extension service, in the problems a farmer faces in making a living on the farm. These are essentially *educational* problems.

When we chose this course TVA knew the state agricultural college and county agent system not only had strengths but faults and weaknesses as well. We were aware of the drag and inertia against new ideas that a long tradition imposes upon an educational institution. We knew that many counties in the Tennessee Valley had no county agents at all; that in some cases where there were county agents they were in reality agents only of the more well-to-do farmers. We knew of the weaknesses. But we were confronted with a choice between systems.

Once we had made our choice—to encourage the state and local system—we deliberately developed and shaped the program for which we were responsible so that it would help the college and its extension system become stronger and more fully aware of how each state and county agency could increase its effectiveness in the job of building the whole region.

As we gained experience under this alliance we saw more and more clearly that we were undertaking a bigger and more fundamental task than that of aiding the farmer to get a higher income. That bigger job was to help make it possible, by the decentralization methods we espoused, for the people to understand the dangers of excessive economic and administrative centralization which some assert these days (falsely, as I believe) is the price we all must pay for advance in science and technical knowledge.

Another illustration of decentralization is afforded by the TVA's power system. TVA has a system of more than a score of dams on the Tennessee River. Those structures carry out the familiar Federal responsibilities of the de-

velopment of navigation and flood control on an inter-
state river. They provide a navigable channel now being
put to extensive use by the barges of commerce and also a
measure of flood control unprecedented in this country.
The same structures through their control of water gen-
erate huge amounts of electricity.

Congress directed that that electricity should be sold.
Among private companies it is customary for electricity
to be generated, transmitted, and distributed to the homes
and farms and factories by a single concern. In the Tennessee Valley, however, the disposition of electricity is
divided up. The TVA, a central agency, operates the generating plants and thousands of miles of transmission
lines. The distribution of electricity, however, is decentralized. More than a hundred and forty locally owned,
locally managed, locally financed distribution agencies
carry the electricity from the city gates, where TVA de-
livers it wholesale in bulk, to the ultimate consumers.

Here again an alternative was found to centralized administration. An agreement between TVA, the Federal
agency, and these many cities, towns, and rural cooperatives, fixes broad general policies of accounting, general
financial policy, and tax payments, and determines the
level of consumer rates, subject to mutual adjustment.
But the administration of electricity supply has been
effectively decentralized.

Part of TVA's task is to aid in the development of
private industry through research and exploration of the
natural resources of the region so that they can serve in
raising the level of income and the level of economic

activity of the citizens of the region. This, too, as everyone knows, is not a novel function of the Federal government. One recalls that the Department of Commerce, the Department of Agriculture, the bureaus of the Department of the Interior, and others have had comparable objectives and responsibilities for a considerable number of years.

These research and resource development activities of TVA are as fully as possible carried out by a combination of TVA sponsorship with actual execution in whole or part by various state agencies. As a matter of legal authority all such activities might have been carried out by the TVA directly.

In pursuing these decentralizing methods, the TVA has encountered and continues today to encounter a great deal of resistance. There are those who would like to take over one or another phase of TVA's function and put it into some centralized Federal bureau—in the interest, so we are repeatedly told, of uniformity. But surely uniformity is not an end in itself, disregarding that diversity which is one of the great sources of our national strength.

Overcentralization is tempting to many. It has a special appeal to the administrator who quite conscientiously sees the complexity of his job in a coast-to-coast responsibility. The oversimplifications and the uniform rules and regulations which centralization encourages, are convenient for him, however inconvenient it may be for the public.

There are those in Congress and among Federal administrators who quite genuinely doubt whether they can discharge the Federal responsibilities for nation-wide programs and for Federal funds (such as those in aid of education) if they must rely upon local units of government over which there does not exist the authority to hire and fire and to set and enforce Washington "standards."

It seems to me however that as against the folly of centralized administration the risks involved in delegations and agreements with state and local agencies seem clearly preferable. Indeed, are not these risks implicit in our democratic faith?

Nor should we overlook the deeper question of how we can help our state and local government gain in competence and in capacity. Surely we should not encourage state and local governments to escape from their duties or abdicate their responsibilities to Big Government, for this is a process that perpetuates whatever are the local weaknesses.

To turn administration of localized problems over to Washington on the ground that thus we escape the inefficiencies and political shenanigans of state and local communities, is nonsense. It merely transfers the political pressures from local into Federal political channels. Moreover, centralization to avoid unsavory local influences surely deprives the people of the chance to draw their issues locally and to clean up their own local inadequacies. The fundamental solution is to crowd more, not less responsibility into the community. Only as the consequences of administrational errors become more localized, can we expect citizens to know which rabbit to shoot.

Overcentralized administration is not something simply to be made more palatable, more efficient, and better managed. It is a hazard to democracy. It is a hazard to freedom. Centralization at the national capital or in a business undertaking always glorifies the importance of pieces of paper. This dims the sense of reality. As men and organizations acquire a preoccupation with papers, they become less understanding, less perceptive of the reality of those matters with which they should be dealing: particular human problems, particular human beings, actual things in a real America—highways, wheat, barges, drought, floods, backyards, blast furnaces. The facts with which a highly centralized institution deals tend to be the men and women of that institution itself, and their ideas and ambitions. To maintain perspective and human understanding in the atmosphere of centralization is a task that many able and conscientious people have found well-nigh impossible.

Many administrators recognize this simple truth. But we are so prone to accept Big Government, to improve and refine it at the center to the sad neglect of the periphery where the people live and work, that the Federal administrator who tries to reverse the trend is hailed as the exception to the rule. I cite one noteworthy illustration—there are many more. The Secretary of the Interior, Hon. J. A. Krug, has urged the creation of a decentralized regional agency, to aid in the unified development of the Columbia River Valley. In explaining the decentralizing consequences of this proposal Secretary Krug has said: "Final decisions would be made here in the Northwest instead of in my Department in Washington. I would like to give up some of my power and authority exercised at Washington and see it exercised here." In such a spirit of self-imposed restraint among administrators and in Congress lies the road to a workable alternative to Big Government.

Big Government will get bigger and more highly centralized unless there is a conscious, continuous, creative administrative and legislative effort to reverse the trend. The community's impulse to hand its local problems over piecemeal to one remote agency after another, feeds this hazardous push toward Big Government. The surrender of local responsibility for a part of the community's function generates further local weaknesses which furnish the reason for yet another surrender. Local communities and state governments can help by resisting these temptations to take the easy way out. They can help the administrators of Federal programs to work out the methods of decentralization case by case.

Those who believe devoutly in the democratic process should be the first to urge the use of methods that will keep the administration of national functions from becoming so concentrated at the national capital, so distant from the everyday life of ordinary people as to wither and deaden the average citizen's sense of participation and partnership in government affairs. For it is this citizen participation that nourishes the strength of a democracy.

9. UNIVERSAL PUBLIC SERVICE: A PROPOSAL

Universal Public Service:
A Proposal

OUR concept of what constitutes a decent society, our deepest moral convictions and our ideas of self-government are today the targets of a fanatical extremism. This is not a crisis of a few months or even a few years' duration; in all probability we face a generation of almost unrelieved tension.

Such a trial will call for steadfastness and faith. It will moreover require that we exhibit the very greatest skills in self-government, solid judgment and open-mindedness in the development of public policies, and creativeness in all the arts of government. As we chart our course through these dark waters our very survival will require that our public servants be something better than political hangers-on or plodding mediocrities: we shall need the very best of a wide spectrum of talents the country affords.

In these circumstances I am convinced that the method of manning the public service (if indeed something so casual and hit-or-miss can be called a "method") that may have worked not too badly in less exacting times must be drastically modified. It seems to me that a moral obligation to engage in the public service during a part of every qualified man's best years has become, for the gen-

eration that lies ahead, an actual necessity; that there
must be an increased movement into the public service
from private pursuits by exceptionally qualified people
who would not in ordinary times consider public service
as any part of their life's work; it is equally important that
we put increased emphasis on rotation in the public service, in order to augment the flow into private responsibility of men with knowledge of government gained from
actual experience.

Intense but sporadic manifestations of interest in government, such as are exhibited during the excitement of a
major political campaign, are not adequate to insure the
workability of representative democracy either in community affairs or in national domestic concerns; they are
quite clearly inadequate for the demands put upon our
government by the increased importance of science and
by the role of world leadership that is now ours. It seems
to me that the true measure of the importance people at-
tach to government is evidenced by every individual's
sense of his duties and obligations as a citizen; or to put
it another way, by the moral purposes and convictions and
the underlying philosophy of each generation.

When my generation was graduated from college, in
the twenties, we had a rather definite philosophy which
can be summed up in this phrase: "Take care of Number
One."

The idea was a simple one; it was almost universally
accepted; it seemed eminently sensible. If everyone de
voted himself to his own success, to his own advancement,

if everyone took care of Number One, and concentrated on that, obviously the sum total of the successes of all the Number Ones would be prosperity and happiness all around, an end to poverty, in brief, a golden era.

"Taking care of Number One" was not confined to individuals, and the careers of individuals. It applied to groups. If farmers looked out for their own interests, if organized labor and industrial management did the same for their respective interests, if physicians and lawyers and bankers and bond salesmen and shipbuilders and merchants, each looked out for Number One, then all the Number Ones would be looked out for.

The same philosophy dominated international relations of the twenties. If the United States concentrated on advancing the welfare of the United States, and if Germany did the same, and Britain the same, and France and Russia and all the other nations, then by the philosophy of "Look out for Number One," by each nation paying strict attention to its own business, the sum total would be prosperity and peace for all.

The idea seemed sound; it was what we then liked to call "just plain common sense." We had made the simple discovery that not only was poverty unnecessary but so was war. To make sure of it, all the Number Ones—who were each going to look out for themselves—got together and signed an eloquent piece of paper—the Kellogg Pact —agreeing that there would be no more wars.

For a time the idea of looking out for Number One was surprisingly profitable. It was, by and large, a time of easy earning and free spending. In our naïveté, we attributed our easy success to our own great talents for money-making, and to the fine education in self-advancement we had received from the universities of the land.

Nations found the idea worked well, too. We protected our own industries by high tariffs, and other nations took measures they deemed appropriate to take care of their prosperity. Taxes were low, and the budget was balanced. There was no need for expensive armies and navies, since we had a piece of paper that said, officially, that war had been outlawed. With every interest watching out for its own pickings, the President could take a long nap every afternoon, and Congress a rest several months out of every term.

But to say that "Taking care of Number One" *did not work* is a masterpiece of understatement. Judged by the implacable and merciless test of results—a prostrating depression followed by a terrible war—it was soon made clear that the philosophy of my generation was somehow tragically in error.

The arts of self-government, the whole process of government that had seemed so irrelevant, so inconsequential to us who thought we had found the golden way, became suddenly the center of our greatest concern. Many of our leading citizens, who had never before given a thought to government except as a minor irritation, gave up their business to devote themselves entirely to government, in order to pull us out of economic havoc. Later they put their own interests aside to work in government in order to help win a war, a war their own sons were fighting.

Some of our generation, thinking it over later, felt that it might have been better if they had concerned themselves with government sooner. They wondered if it wouldn't have been smarter to have come to Washington, or to have concerned themselves more with the kind of men chosen to go to Washington, before depression and war were upon us.

We have done some sober thinking since the good old days of the twenties when we worshiped at the altar of Personal Success. And we can't honestly recommend "Take care of Number One" as a philosophy for the present generation. What I propose in its stead I can compress in this phrase:

"Be an active, living part of the times."

Do a good job and attain success in a chosen field. Be self-reliant, but not self-sufficient, self-centered, self-loving. Becoming an active part of the times I propose as the best, though clearly a most difficult, alternative to the idea of each man withdrawing into the shell of self-preoccupation, of concern solely about his own success.

I can best suggest what I have in mind by quoting the remarks of two men.

Warren Gamaliel Harding, twenty-eighth President of the United States, exemplified to a degree the central philosophy of the generation of the twenties, a generation that with infinite appropriateness made him and his associates our corporeal and symbolic leaders. President Harding is reported to have said: "Government, after all, is a simple thing."

Next I quote the comment of Dr. Albert Einstein,

whose brain has comprehended abstractions and ara-
besques of the intellect quite beyond most of us:
"Politics," the great mathematician said, meaning, I take
it, the whole art of government, "is more difficult than
physics." And for physics I think we may substitute
science, all science.

The times will be chiefly occupied with these two:
physics and politics, or more accurately, science and government.

When I urge that everyone play an active part in science, I do not, of course, suggest that the members of this
generation must all adopt science and engineering as a
life's work. What I do urge is that, as educated citizens,
that is to say privileged citizens, they keep informed of the
essentials, of the basic facts. For it is chiefly upon the lay
citizen, informed about science but not its practitioner,
that the country must depend in determining *the use to
which science is put,* in resolving the many public policy
questions that scientific discoveries constantly force upon
us. These are matters largely for the good judgment, in
human affairs, of all citizens, scientists and non-scientists.

Now, as to being active in government, do I mean what
we call "good citizenship," that is keeping informed on
public questions by reading and listening to the radio and
attending forums, by remembering to vote, and never
neglecting to put the wastepaper neatly at the curb during
Clean-Up-Your-Town Week? That will not be enough,
not for what the American people are going to encounter
in the fifties of this century.

In the next three decades I urge that every educated

person, who is qualified to do so, plan definitely to set aside a number of years for the rendering of service in the legislative or executive branches of his local, state or Federal government.

I am, in fact, proposing a wide-spread rotation of the not-too-pleasant duties of the public service. And I do not mean merely part-time or "dollar-a-year" service alone. Nor in my opinion will it meet the situation to put this public service off until retirement age.

I propose that, out of the best and most productive years of each man's life, he should carve a segment in which he puts his private career aside to serve his community and his country, and thereby to serve his children, his neighbors, his fellow-men, and the cause of freedom.

By whom should the public services be manned? By mediocrity and by hacks? Or by our very ablest citizens? I say it must be the latter, and it is for that reason I make this proposal of a citizen Universal Public Service.

In the twenties, in the Era of Common Sense, government was something way off yonder, something really quite unimportant. We were well content to permit people we thought not quite respectable, or not quite good enough for the competitive struggle, to run government. Rarely did we come to the aid of the many fine, able men in public service.

In those days our own careers were what counted. Why in the world should anyone break into his career to associate with a bunch of politicos in the city council, or the state legislature, or in Congress? We would have asked, in some indignation: What sense does it make for a fine physician to bother with veterans' hospitals, or a distinguished scientist or engineer to bother trying to give special quality to a government research laboratory, or a rising young business executive to bring modern ideas of management into public works? That just wouldn't have made sense.

We were sensible in the twenties. Government wasn't important, we thought, and by the time we found out that we were wrong, it was late, very late indeed.

I urge this generation not to drift into the same error. I say that there is no one in this country, however talented, however well trained, however ambitious, who can safely adopt the attitude toward local or Federal government, in all its many ramifications, that we of the twenties adopted.

Upon the ability and integrity and judgment of men and women in government—whether they be mediocre and mere "good fellows" and windbags, or whether they be talented, well trained and independent—too many grave decisions depend these days to permit anyone to assert that his career is too important to be bothered by the irrelevance of government service.

We all remember with pride that in the early formative years of the Republic, full-time public service, though at least as distasteful as today, was not thought beneath the talents or the dignity of the ablest and most successful of men. By any measure Mr. Washington and Mr. Jefferson were not the least able citizens of their communities.

The maintenance of peace? Is that important to us as individuals? To our children?

Business stability—or depression? Is that important: I mean important to each individual?

Sensible taxation and fiscal policies—or the kind that bankrupt us? World trade—or a contracting economic isolation? Scientific progress, outdistancing the world, or the hamstringing of scientific enterprise? Public education on a flourishing basis, or in a state of collapse?

Are these things important to this generation? By and large most of these questions are determined, the course laid out, by men in the public service. They had better be the best men and women we have, since these are among the most important questions we have.

I do not urge that everyone pursue public service, in some form, as a life career. I am inclined to think that the idea of public service *as a life-time career* has certain severe limitations, judged by present-day public needs.

Here I differ with some students of public affairs: it seems to me that the advantages of the permanent-career public service are customarily overstated, in the light of our own American needs, and that the disadvantages have not been sufficiently understood.

What I urge is a fluid kind of citizen-service, in which men and women move from private life into public service for a period of years, and then back to private life. Thus there will be an almost ideal situation, as I see it, in this: On their return to private life, these citizens will be experienced in firsthand knowledge of public affairs and of the special difficulties that beset the public servant; we will have public servants whose judgment will be enriched by recent experience in the day-to-day problems of private affairs.

Such a plan has a number of advantages to the country. The proposal also has in it an element of common fairness, for the grim and wearing tasks that so often are the lot of the responsible public servant should not be exacted of one man for an indefinite period, but should be deliberately rotated.

Policy-making officials are, quite naturally, subject to constant pressures and often violent criticism designed to induce, persuade, or intimidate them into seeing issues as their critics do. From the point of view of the whole public it seems to me that men in such posts should not be encouraged in any way to regard security of position or lengthy tenure as their lot. On the contrary they should regard it as quite normal to resign or retire when they find it no longer possible to do what they believe is a good job. The "place-holder" psychology among men in policy or high administrative responsibility breeds a kind of chronic expediency, and a caution and timidity inconsistent with the public interest in times such as these.

The "rotation" or fluid public-service idea here advanced is, generally speaking, better calculated to produce the requisite independence in our public servants, as compared with that emphasis on security and stability implicit in the "career" service concept.

The line between the responsibilities of private business executives and of policy officials in government was once very clear: one was engaged in private pursuits, the other in public. Today this line is no longer clear. The *public* responsibilities of large-scale private business are so extensive that top executives spend much of their time upon issues quite similar to those that chiefly occupy the attention of many public servants. Conversely, more and more government executives are now engaged upon work that is largely of a business character, ranging from huge industrial or construction operations to vast financial or insurance enterprises, wherein business considerations and techniques are of high importance. The fact is that businessmen, in large enterprise today, are more nearly like public servants, and public servants more like businessmen, than ever before.

This striking new development is an added reason supporting this proposal. Business—with its public character—can become better adapted to its public responsibilities by a regular inflow of men with government experience, as government, with its strong preoccupation with business problems and methods will be better adapted to the demands made upon it if there is a continual inflow of men with experience in private business.

This proposal for universal public service presents a number of practical difficulties, although none of them seem to me insurmountable. It is also subject to a number of objections: for example, that individuals could enter the public service for the purpose of benefiting the private business to which they expect to return in a number of years; or that men in government, expecting to be in the public employment only a few years could misuse their position to cultivate the good will of prospective private employers. But, unhappily, this is a situation that has long existed; it might, in fact, be somewhat less common as a consequence of a changed public attitude toward government which wide-spread adoption of this proposal might well develop. None of the various objections compare in importance to the necessity for this changed attitude toward the public service. With a change in that basic philosophy, then an atmosphere will have been created in which the practical difficulties and objections to the proposal, while they will not disappear entirely, will certainly be quite manageable.

I have confidence that the philosophy of "Take care of Number One" has so clearly been demonstrated a tragic failure that it will not be embraced again by this generation; that despite occasional (and quite human) relapses from time to time we will not again be led down that road. I firmly believe that this generation intends to be and will become an active living part of its times.

10. UTILITY MANAGE-
MENT—A PUBLIC
TRUST

Utility Management — A Public Trust

THE safeguarding and stimulation of economic opportunity has been an accepted function of governmental leadership since the first days of the Republic. That fact of our history is too often buried beneath floods of nostalgic oratory, pleading for an early return to a Never-Never Land of Pure Free Enterprise, a state that like the Emerald City of Oz never did exist. From the days of Alexander Hamilton and the first "protective" tariff, designed to build up New England factories and thereby the national well-being, to the granting of an airline certificate to protect an aviation company from uneconomic competition, government has always been called upon to intervene in the development of private business. Time and again Congress has acted to restrict the freedom of action of one kind of business enterprise in order that the freedom of other businesses might be widened.

As we look back today we see that some of these governmental acts proved to be not in the general public interest. Others were wise and productive. Almost invariably, however, when any branch of government has acted to protect, to promote, to discourage or restrict business, it has had to justify its action and it has had public support only where the objective could be shown to be the general good.

Nor is it true, as is often asserted, that all our hopes of expansion and increased production depend solely and exclusively upon private business and that government never produces or adds to our economic wealth. This ignores facts of common observation. The automobile industry is an outstanding and a proud example of private enterprise; the modern highways of the United States are a spectacular illustration of public business. Both are equally a manifestation of the American spirit of enterprise; both are productive. The true relation of these two undertakings is illuminated by the fact that without modern highways, which could only have been financed and built by the public, the brilliant record of private enterprise in the automobile industry would never have been written; and, of course, without the automobile pioneers, the modern highways would not be needed and would not in fact exist.

The issue of governmental action versus simon pure free enterprise is an imaginary one. The real issue is, does a *particular* governmental action promote and protect economic opportunity for the whole people? In the long run is all enterprise, private and public, promoted by the particular governmental intervention or activity under discussion?

A good illustration is afforded by the relation between government and the private companies supplying elec-

tricity, gas, transportation, and so on, in short the public
utilities. Many years ago Professor Frederick W. Taussig
of Harvard said:

It is not too much to say the future of democracy will
depend on its success in dealing with the problems of public
ownership and regulation. To allow the great monopoly
industries to remain without control in private hands is to
allow an *imperium in imperio*—nothing less than a plu-
tocracy. To manage them as public enterprises, or to regu-
late them effectively while still in private hands, calls for
restraint, abdication of the town-meeting method, intelligence in choosing good leaders, steadfastness in following
them. These things are not learned in a day.

Much of the difficulty in thinking clearly on the relations between a democratic government and the public
utilities, in my judgment, arises out of the fact that we
have not kept in mind just what kind of businesses these
public utilities are after all.

A public utility enterprise, though privately owned, is
a hybrid, a cross between public and private enterprise.
It is not precisely like an ordinary private business, and
it only invites confusion to think of it as such. There is
really no such thing as a "private" utility. The term is
"public" utility, whether the utility in question is owned
and operated by private persons or owned by the public
and operated by public officials.

The fact that the functions of public utilities are not
performed by public officials and the financing is not
derived from the public treasury but from private indi-

viduals does not change the nature of the functions which they perform. What is more important, it does not change the essential relation between the government and the public utilities which are acting for the organized community of citizens in performing these public services.

The prevailing practice in this country is that government (local or Federal) is not the owner, operator, and banker for public utility enterprises but the regulator.

The purpose of regulation, as I conceive of it, is simply to see to it that the public utility corporations which perform an indispensable public function for the community shall be so operated as to benefit the community. To be of benefit to the community they must be treated by the public authorities and in legislation with scrupulous fairness, in a financial sense, for an almost insolvent and impoverished company cannot render good service.

When these private-public businesses depart from the objective of community service the community through its government must step in and demand correctives, just as it would or should do if the operators of a publicly-owned enterprise, such as the post office, or a municipal power system, were to run that business for personal or political profit, with public service secondary.

The ownership and management of a utility, like the holding of a public office, is a public trust. The ownership of capital in a public utility enterprise does not therefore carry with it the right to earn speculative profits, and those who hope for such profits must turn to some other of the many lines of endeavor where such profits are legitimate.

Investments in privately owned utilities are entitled to protection. No one wants uneconomic competition or the waste of duplicating facilities. But privately owned utilities to whom territorial or business exclusive rights have been given by government have an obligation, in turn, to deal fairly with the community, to recognize that the public interest is paramount. In one of the first cases which came before the Supreme Court of the United States involving the claims of a public utility to a monopoly, Mr. Chief Justice Taney said: "While the rights of private property are sacredly guarded, we must not forget that the community also have rights, and that the happiness and well-being of every citizen depends on their faithful preservation."

A public opinion must be developed which will make it just as heinous a civic offense to debauch such a public business as it is to use trust funds for private gain. Effective regulation, strict securities laws we must have, but above and beyond them must be a militant public opinion which declares: "Public utilities must be conducted as a public trust, for the benefit of the community they serve."

By its very nature, the business of generation and distribution of electricity is a public business, because in our present-day community life we are all dependent upon that service. It is in large measure due to electric power that for the first time in the history of civilization man has the potential capacity to produce enough commodities to supply the population with the necessities and even many of the luxuries.

We are well along the road to a mastery of production, and yet we are just at the beginning of this power age. The future possibilities are as limitless as the imagination of our scientists and the ingenuity of our inventors. No wonder, then, that it is so vital that the community maintain an effective, realistic, nonpolitical control over these great natural resources of energy. In another twenty years or so a wholly new source of energy from the heart of the atom will be added to our existing vast sources of electricity.

Electricity has become a symbol of freedom from drudgery, of a new way of living. Electricity is a symbol as a flag is a symbol. Matter-of-fact people might say: "After all, what is the American flag? Simply a piece of colored cloth. What is there about cloth for people to get emotional about?" Such a remark is foolish, of course. It is just as foolish to try to wave aside deep issues involved in power by saying that electricity is just one other thing people buy, just as they buy a carton of cigarettes, or to say that in point of fact electricity is actually a small part of the family budget, a statement which is true in a literal sense, but quite wrong in every other way.

The fact is that the rank and file of people look upon electricity as a force that, properly released, can change the whole face of living for themselves and their children. We can hardly think how life would go on, certainly in a city or town, without electricity. Almost every day science and invention are finding new uses for this energy. Most of us remember the time when electricity meant a light bulb hanging from a cord. That was considered a kind of minor miracle then, and so it was.

Today we do not think of electricity as a naked light bulb. In millions of homes over a slender wire comes music and the news of the world and living pictures. From that same wire comes heat for cooking, and cold for refrigeration, energy to wash clothes and pump water. In our factories electricity brings power to run the tiniest motor or to move huge machinery. It does more than this. It brings new and incalculable forces into play that will determine the kind of country we will live in a decade or two hence.

In the earlier days of our so-called "machine age" it was the steam engine that stood like a magnetic force at the very center of things. Since the power of the steam engine could not be broken up and sent out to the worker, men and women were brought into factories concentrated in a few large industrial centers. To a certain extent the earlier technical advance of American industry was paid for at the expense of the worker's welfare. All too often he got the short end of technical advance in the steam engine days.

Electricity can change and is changing this. It is a flexible and mobile force. It can move out, coursing over transmission networks, to seek the worker at the factory, the quarry, and the mine. As much as any other single force, it can help and is helping to eliminate the sweatshop and the slum, to restore a balance of opportunity between city and country, between the factory and the farm.

Electricity on the farm can be not only a principal

source of additional income to the farmer; it can be an energizing force, not only literally but in its impact on farming as a way of living. I once accompanied the late Senator George W. Norris on a visit to the home of a farmer living not far from Wilson Dam, who until the then very recent construction of a line by TVA had not had electricity on his place. The *Chattanooga News* of November 25, 1935 reported the incident in this way:

Weatherbeaten and sadly in need of paint, the house was located in the midst of fertile acres that stretched around. Through the house the farmer conducted them. Here he pointed to his water heater, his glistening white refrigerator, his lights and other appliances newly installed. At the back door he pridefully called his visitors' attention to a water pump, operated by electricity, like other appliances in his house. Then he grew a little apologetic. "This house here doesn't look like much," he said. "It's in need of some paint, and repairs. But now we've got electricity in here, we're planning to fix up things. We're going to do over the place, maybe add some rooms."

There is nothing complicated or technical about the basic issues concerning electricity. We need not try to follow through the maze of technical discussions by engineers, accountants, and rate experts. One principle we must understand: Electricity is the people's business. The rest in a sense is detail. The business of supplying electricity must be run by those who deem themselves servants of the community, whether as officers of private corporations or as public officials. Otherwise the full benefits that can flow from electricity will never come to us and to our children.

The supply of electricity began years ago largely as a local enterprise. Throughout the country, separate electric generating plants and distribution facilities were set up in each community. Frequently they were built and operated by cities and towns themselves. Generally, however, the privilege of furnishing electricity was conferred on corporations, whose supervision, even in the larger communities, was for the most part in the hands of the people in the community itself. Then came a great engineering development. It proved to be more economical to send the electricity from a few large plants over high-power transmission lines into a whole group of communities than to use small local plants, each operating separately.

What changed the characteristics of the electricity business, however, was not only this engineering development but the influence of the financier. The rabbit which he pulled out of his hat was the holding company. In ten to fifteen years most of the people's business of electricity left the actual control of local ownership or regulation and became concentrated in the financial centers of our country.

In this process of concentration and financial exploitation, electricity was usually not dealt with as a public enterprise and a great social force. During that period the dominant elements of the public utility industry did not, nor did its controlling financial interests permit it to, devote itself primarily to its basic function of making

more and more electricity available at the lowest feasible
cost to the American home and to industry. Here was a
serious failure, for monopolies were granted to electric
utilities solely because it was thought that in this way electricity would cost the consumer less than under competitive conditions. There could have been no other justification.

Fair rates, proper accounting, preventing stock swin-
dles, limiting holding company transactions—all these
are important. But they are only part of the problem of
strengthening practical and workable public control, according to democratic principle, of this essential of life.

The problem is, in part, one of decentralizing and
localizing that part of electricity administration which
deals intimately with human beings, and to centralize
those functions in which economies can be effected by
large-scale central administration, but in which little or
no contact and no day-to-day relations with the public
are involved.

The generation of electricity is an out-and-out
engineering matter and a central organization is the best
way to do it. Transmission—carrying power on a network from remote powerhouses to city gates—is another
instance in which centralization is necessary and from
which real efficiencies result. The distribution of that
power within a local community is essentially a local
matter. There it is important that the people who manage the enterprise be local, not someone at the other end
of a long-distance phone.

The technical job of generating and transmitting

power calls for specialized skill and a large organization. The distribution systems themselves in the local community can usually be owned and managed under boards of local citizens. Whether the local system is well or badly administered, whether or not the people reap the full benefits of power development should depend upon the people themselves rather than on some far-off government bureau or remote company executive.

To achieve a workable and fair control of electricity in the hands of the people does not, by any manner of means, require universal public ownership. What it does require is a recognition of the public character of electricity and of the paramount rights of individuals and the community. This process will doubtless be a long one. It takes only a few years to impair such a democratic institution as local control of a public function. It often takes a long, uphill effort to rebuild it.

To me an attractive world is not one dominated by such concepts as "security" or "stability" but rather by one of the great words of the language, "opportunity." Electricity is a symbol of opportunity for men, women, and children everywhere. It gives the farm family opportunity for the conveniences of the city dweller. It gives the forward-looking imaginative young businessman an opportunity to translate his ideas into a new enterprise. It gives the manufacturer in a small community or rural area almost as great advantages, as far as the cost of electricity is concerned, as he would have if his plant were next to a powerhouse. A farmer can put a little motor in his woodshed and produce some small wood product; a merchant in a small crossroads hamlet can put in a grist mill, or a cold-storage plant in connection with his store.

But electricity is not a symbol of opportunity unless it is made widely available; a niggardly use of electricity is the very negation of opportunity. Electric rates should be designed so that progressively they become lower and lower, so that electric energy shall be used more and more widely in the homes, the factories, the farms, and the lives of the people. With the coming of electricity from atomic power such widespread use in a democracy can help make economic opportunity blossom as it never has before in all history.

11 ATOMIC ENERGY—A NEW KIND OF PEOPLE'S BUSINESS

Atomic Energy—A New Kind of People's Business

THE atomic energy program of the United States comprises a huge scientific, technical, industrial, educational, manufacturing and weaponeering enterprise. It reaches from the Belgian Congo in Africa, across the continental United States, to Eniwetok Atoll in the Marshall Islands of the Pacific. More than 60,000 people are employed in it, most of them by private concerns who, under contract, act as operators or agents of the Atomic Energy Commission. They work in laboratories, in chemical plants, in huge production and refining plants, in hospitals and universities. They are at work in most states of the Union, in Tennessee, in New York, in Ohio, on top of a mesa in New Mexico, in California, on the banks of the Columbia River in the State of Washington. Many more people are directly contributing in their work for the hundreds of firms which supply the Commission or its contractors with materials and equipment. And, in addition, there are the explorers, the men engaged in the most intensive search of modern times, the search for uranium, indispensable raw material of atomic energy.

This complex and unique enterprise is the public's

123

business. It is wholly owned by the people of the United States. The reason atomic energy is by law a government undertaking and a government monopoly is an obvious one: its intimate relation to our national defense and security.

But far more is at stake in the atomic energy program than increasing America's military strength. Congress decided after months of hearings and extended public discussion that while atomic energy is of central importance to the national defense, it holds the broadest implications for our health, agriculture, industry, education— for our whole way of life, and for world peace. Therefore it must be fitted into the democratic scheme of civilian self-government through the medium of a Commission responsible not only for progress in weaponeering but in the far broader sphere of nonmilitary potentialities of these great discoveries.

In the opening section of the law creating this civilian Commission Congress made this declaration:

It is hereby declared to be the policy of the people of the United States that, subject at all times to the paramount objective of assuring the common defense and security, the development and utilization of atomic energy shall, so far as practicable, be directed toward improving the public welfare, increasing the standard of living, strengthening free competition in private enterprise and promoting world peace.

In the nonmilitary applications of these discoveries is a whole new technology, ripe for development. From the unfolding knowledge in this new field we may confidently expect new techniques and new industrial processing, leading to basic improvements in existing industrial methods and in time to entirely new industries and new products. The stimulating influence of this new area of industrial knowledge on many sectors of industry quite removed from or remotely related to atomic energy is likely to be very great indeed.

Out of all this will surely come a stronger and more productive industry and business, and therefore the prospect of a stronger people and a stronger country. In this vigorous people and developing country lies the greatest, perhaps the only real physical assurance of, "common defense and security."

Such are the prospects. The early results point to great developments ahead. But there is something here quite unlike anything in our own history of technical development, and contrary to the way in which such revolutionary physical and social changes have evolved in our democratic society.

I refer, of course, to the fact that this huge enterprise is government-owned, as trustee for the people of the United States. Not only that: there appears every prospect that it will continue as an almost wholly publicly owned undertaking and a government monopoly for a considerable time to come.

Why should this be? What are the barriers in the way of developing the atom in accordance with our democratic precepts of diversity and individual competition and risk? Are the barriers real, or are they imagined or manufactured? Why can not these new technical discoveries be developed, and developed rapidly, by the same method that, by and large, this democracy has followed in the past? That method worked for the development of electricity, the telephone, the steam engine, radio, television, the internal combustion engine, chemicals, synthetic materials, and the many other discoveries and developments that have transformed this country and so greatly benefited all of us.

Generally speaking our democratic method has been to follow the path of free inquiry and of competition in ideas. One man's idea competed with another's idea. Private money was risked on the outcome of the competition. The ultimate judge of which is the better idea, whether in chemicals or transportation or the stagecoach, or the automobile or the radio, is the buying and using public. If the idea wins with the public, then those with the best idea are acclaimed, and those who risk their money on that idea stand to profit. If the idea fails to prove out in this buyers' plebiscite, those who put up their money stand to lose it.

In thus describing our course I have oversimplified, but in general that has been the American formula. It has worked wonders, and it continues to do so. All of American basic industry began this way, and except for public utility services, which are now legal monopolies under regulation, American business by and large continues to operate this way. We know that it must be a pretty good way, or the over-all results would not be so good. Those results are good, for they have given us a fabulous productiveness that has not exacted our essential freedoms as its price, but indeed can be made to increase the sum total of freedom of choice for the individual.

As everyone knows the atomic enterprise did not begin in this traditional way. The automobile and the airplane began with puttering in dozens of little bicycle shops. But this technical achievement was a giant at birth, a two billion dollar war-baby, gestated in secrecy and nourished wholly on government money.

When the Atomic Energy Commission assumed responsibility for this enterprise on January 1, 1947, there was turned over to it a nationalized enterprise, owned lock, stock, and barrel by the United States. The Commission's predecessor, the Manhattan Engineer District of the Army, had one purpose and one purpose only: to produce an atomic bomb. It was not the Manhattan District's job to develop any other of the many potentialities of atomic energy. To particular industries had been assigned particular tasks, such as the design, construction, and operation of a plant to separate out Uranium 235 from natural uranium, or to factory-produce the new element Plutonium or to develop and manufacture this or that device, usually without knowing what the whole mechanism was to be used for. These assigned tasks included among them some of the greatest technical achievements of engineering and industrial history. There was no problem of incentives for industry or for scientists. The war supplied the incentive.

The success of the whole wartime mission was an accomplishment of the first magnitude. But it was *not* an example of the development of an industry under the tested American democratic formula. Indeed it was almost the exact opposite.

This secret nationalized industry did a war job. That war job over, Congress spent more than a year studying what was to be done with it. Although it was a Congress by no means disposed toward departing from the usual formula, the conclusion was that at this stage of development the Government must continue to own and to supervise and direct this undertaking.

Why not sell it off to private industry as a surplus war asset, just as with scores of chemical plants and steel mills? With the war out of the way, why not get this new and promising technical development back on the historic track?

What stands in the way is not ideology or doctrine but the facts about nuclear reaction. No arguments about ideology will change those facts. What we have here is a practical question, and not a abstract debate. As a practical problem this is the way it shapes up:

We have something big here, a great asset. That asset is knowledge. It is not just a number of vast buildings and machinery costing billions of dollars. It is not just a stockpile of bombs and fissionable materials. We Americans have a hand-hold on great and new knowledge. We stand in a good position to learn more, and to learn it fast. We have made a beginning in learning how to put what we know to many uses. But by far the most important of these uses are still unseen and unknown.

What is the best way, the quickest way—and most important of all—the characteristically democratic way, of getting the most benefit from this asset of knowledge, for the people of this country and for the peace of the world?

The Atomic Energy Commission's policy and practice as thus far evolved is to seek to develop the many different potentialities of atomic energy and of nuclear reactions in the way that comes closest to the way this country has followed in developing other new fields of knowledge and technical advance. Where we depart from that way the departure should be justified, not by some doctrinaire or abstract reason, but because of the force of the distinctive and special facts about the atom that require such departure.

The objective should be to get the atomic development back into the mainstream of democratic economic life and gradually to denationalize an industry born nationalized. To accomplish this, however, requires that the seed of the atomic power industry be separated from the prickly burr atomic weapons. But this plucking out of atomic power from atomic weapons turns out to be impossible. The impossibility is set, not by ideological or political considerations, but by the very nature of atomic energy itself.

The business of making atomic power happens, unfortunately, to be the same as the business of making atomic bombs, up to a point very far along in the process. In order to maintain government control of atomic weapons, Congress had no choice except to give both the weapon development and the power development to a government agency. It was apparent that where one went, the other had to go.

In administering this people's business the Atomic
Energy Commission does, however, have some room for
choice in deciding whether the work toward an atomic
energy industry shall be carried on chiefly by the Government directly, or chiefly by American industry in a
sense as partners of the Government. The Commission
has pursued the latter course.

It seems clear to me that if the nation is to have the
strongest kind of atomic industry that industry must, like
our other great industries, be the product of the talents
and efforts of a wide sector of the people. We should not
at our peril downgrade the role which private industry
must play as a co-trustee with the Commission in this
development. The Commission's practice has been to
distribute the task in appropriate segments to industry
as well as to educational institutions spread widely over
the nation wherever the required talents and facilities
and interest can be found.

To adapt our tested democratic practices to this difficult test of their flexibility we need a minimum of governmental monopoly and a maximum of nongovernmental activity. Correspondingly, in further accord with
democratic practice the Commission machinery for the
supervision and managing of this huge enterprise should
be as small as it possibly can be, and as decentralized as
possible.

Both in terms of efficiency and of democratic principle,
these policies seem to me clearly right. But they encounter
forceful opposition and sincere criticism from Congres-

sional and other sources, who would describe themselves as "conservative."

It is argued, for example, that since the Government (by reimbursement provisions) pays the wages of the men working in plants operated for the Commission by a private corporation, such men are in reality government employees and should be regarded as such. It is also urged that since "the Government pays all the bills anyway" the Commission end its practice of engaging private concerns to perform parts of the work. While this has some merit, of course, in special instances, as a general proposition it seems quite unsound, and overlooks the far-reaching effects this atomic industry will, in the course of time, have on all industry, and to that extent, upon our whole democratic framework.

The argument is also made by some members of the Congress that where the Commission engages a private corporation to perform part of its own responsibility, it should "keep a tight control" on that corporation, or as it has been expressed, the Commission's function should be that of "policing" the private concern since it is spending government dollars. Controls such as those the Commission now exercises are essential, obviously; but as a matter of emphasis the point seems dangerously in error.

The major purpose of the Commission's policies should be not the negative ones of "checking" and "policing" but the creation of positive incentives that will stimulate private concerns to carry increasingly larger responsibility. Only in this way, in the long run, can great technical progress be made, dollar costs cut, and the unfortunate consequences of this necessary departure from our traditional industrial course be minimized. A policeman is hardly the man to stir industry to such achievements as have already been recorded by the Commission's industrial partners.

Atomic science is an ever-changing field. What we have in the way of plants may be obsolete tomorrow; indeed it should be a measure of our success that we develop new and better ways that will make today's plants and processes obsolete.

What knowledge we have is not the kind of secret that can be put in an envelope and locked in a vault, and thereby kept as our sole possession for all time. The scientific basis of nuclear energy release is not an American monopoly but is part of a basic store of knowledge that is world-wide. Other nations, including Russia, on their own, will in time learn what we know today.

There are in this country the scientific talents required to continue and strengthen our leadership in atomic energy developments. We have the human skills—engineering, industrial, and managerial—to keep our lead and greatly to increase it. But there is a genuine threat to America's ability to hold on to our world leadership in atomic development, both in weapons and in nonmilitary fields.

This threat to our atomic future grows out of the fact that the huge and complex technical enterprise necessary to produce and improve these weapons is a Federal government activity.

The conditions of work in the Federal government are not attractive. They are becoming increasingly less attractive to many of the very men of managerial and technical skills upon whom our world atomic leadership depends. If one could assume that this is a temporary situation, or were due to the occasionally tawdry tactics or incredible ignorance of a few, then this would not cause much concern. But this is not in fact the situation.

The Federal public service is becoming increasingly unattractive and even repugnant to many specially qualified men for what appear to me to be rather deep-seated reasons. If low salaries, lack of tenure, and occasional intemperate attacks were the only things to be borne they would not in themselves raise such a serious question about the future of the atomic development. For there are able men with sufficient sense of humor, perspective, and devotion to their country who would continue to put up with these handicaps, and without feeling they were entitled to any special credit for so doing.

The difficulties, however, are more fundamental. They consist in the growing evidence that a tendency toward detailed Congressional supervision of this and other essentially technical undertakings make the doing of a creditable job quite impossible.

The price democracy exacts for her benefits is not high for men deeply committed to her cause. When the public task undertaken, however, is made impossible of accomplishment by the increased worsening of the conditions surrounding government service, and men and organiza-

tions find their efforts quite futile, they then will leave
that service, or decline to enter.

It is not only in the development of this new technology, under government auspices, that we face this danger
of abandoning the people's business to the mediocre and
the spineless. For much the same reasons a dark cloud
hangs over the conduct of our world-wide economic activities in the fight for peace and against the spread of
communism. A comparable hazard is to be found affecting important elements of our technical development in
military and civil areas of government activity.

We face this danger chiefly because in recent years
Congress has more and more tended to depart from a
basic principle of our Constitution, the separation of the
legislative from executive or management functions.

At the very period in our history when Congress has
authorized Government to engage in economic and
scientific activities hitherto quite outside the sphere of
Government, Congress has more and more tended to assume detailed, item by item control and therefore management of programs which under the Constitution it is
the function of the President and his appointees of the
Executive branch to carry out. This development has
bred delays, dilution of responsibility, mixing of politics
into technical matters, where it has no place whatever,
and general frustration. It is my observation that it is
this tendency that in large measure accounts for the growing unattractiveness of the Federal service to superior
men. And this comes at the very time when the Executive branch of our democracy has the greatest need in all

our history for the ablest men and women, independent individuals of high talents and devotion to duty, able to carry the unprecedented demands of this period.

It has always been regarded as one of the soundest principles of our democratic system and of our Constitution, as well as an elementary precept of business management, that the fixing of broad policy, and the carrying out of that policy should be kept clearly separated. In the Atomic Energy Act, Congress determined the policy of atomic development. It can, by amendments, revise that policy in general or in detail. However, the carrying forward of the technical development, subject to those policies, and with funds appropriated for that purpose by the Congress, is according to all our traditions the function of the President, acting through individuals appointed by him and confirmed by the Senate. When the Congress, the policy-making body, undertakes to supervise or direct in detail the actual carrying out of the program by the Commission or its industrial agents, or to manage the enterprise by detailed conditions placed upon how the funds appropriated shall be expended, a bewildering confusion of function is introduced. Such a condition will inevitably break the back of the atomic energy enterprise of this country.

In wartime, Congress appropriated two billion dollars without being told what the Manhattan District was about. That was a bizarre extreme which has no possible justification in peacetime, if indeed it had in wartime, no matter how secret the technical aspects must be kept. But because we once followed this one extreme, we should not, at the peril of the health of our atomic undertaking, move toward the other extreme, of a detailed Congressional control and management, which is neither sound in management or constitutional principle, nor workable in practice.

The ablest men cannot be expected nor will they work long under synthetic conditions that in their very nature prevent the doing of good, effective work; this applies with particular force in the secret atomic enterprise where public antagonism and fear and suspicion may be so easily whipped up by jittery or irresponsible men, and where the penalty for failure to do a good job (for whatever reason) is a severe one.

I hope that the trend of the last decade will be reversed. I hope that it will be seen that the field of policy determination, in its broadest aspects, is not only the constitutional role of the Congress, but that as the most important function assigned to any one of the three branches of Government, it should not be mingled with the separate and lesser function of execution.

The only real assurance, however, that the tendency will be reversed lies with public opinion. For without a public opinion alive to the importance of this new technical development, and articulate about the dangers of confusion and frustration of which I write, there is, I believe, less than a bright prospect for the future of atomic development in the United States.

This country has what it takes to keep ahead of the Russians in both military and benign fields of atomic research development. We have what it takes to keep ourselves, in various ways, so very far ahead of them as to add greatly to our security and to the peace of the world during a difficult period of world transition. We shall be able to make that lead so great, in the next few years, as to help provide grave deterrents to aggression. Our position can be made such as will, in a sense, buy time in which to work out a sensible diminution of tensions, and realistic and honorable adjustments.

This can be done. But it will take the American first team to do it, and it will take conditions in the Federal government that will keep the first team in the game.

If the American people are not acutely aware of the vital importance of this technical development to them, to their children, to their security, there is a real hazard that neither our great scientific talents, nor engineering nor administrative skills nor huge sums of appropriated funds can maintain the kind of indisputable and unquestioned atom lead in the world we need. Red tape, bureaucratic frustrations, petty politics, dull, cautious, unimaginative direction will move in and change the whole atmosphere from one of pioneering to dull routine. Drive and intensity, initiative, a sense of urgency will die overnight in such an atmosphere. Top scientists will turn to other lines of inquiry; good administrators will have nothing to do with such an enterprise. It will become a fine nesting place for industrious mediocrity. America's great lead may soon dwindle.

The people must understand what is at stake, and how rapid technical progress in their behalf is made—and how it can be unmade.

12. THE ATOM CAN BE USED TO STRENGTHEN DEMOCRACY

The Atom Can Be Used to Strengthen Democracy

I T WAS the free democracies of Britain, Canada, and the United States and not the totalitarian regimes that developed the greatest force of destruction in all the history of warfare. Will this great achievement of wartime turn upon us, and actually weaken rather than strengthen the forces of democracy? Wellington, reviewing a new contingent of tough and hardy troops, is reported to have said, "I do not know how the enemy will feel about these terrific fellows—but they frighten me." Have we cause to be in fear of the effect on our democratic future of our own accomplishment?

Many thoughtful men have felt, from the very day of the drop on Hiroshima, and still feel, that atomic discoveries, though originating with us, are more a cause for fear than for confidence for the future of free institutions.

They have many things in mind in expressing these concerns and conclusions. Secrecy and democracy are not compatible, they say, nor can they be made compatible, whereas secrecy flourishes in a totalitarian state. If we in America are forced to pursue atomic secrecy, secrecy will spread to other areas, and in no time at all will fasten its evil consequences upon our whole life. We shall thus drive ourselves away from that openness that is so characteristic of democratic practice and belief. The atom bomb, they go on to point out, increases the value of surprise attack. The launching of a surprise attack is not something a democracy can do; it is only a totalitarian system that can use it to advantage. Russia in time will have a stockpile of these weapons, so useful for surprise. We shall be then at a great disadvantage as a democracy. The pressure to equalize the situation by moving away from our cherished democracy will not be one we can afford to resist, if we would survive. Further, it is said, preoccupation with warfare is a characteristic not of democracy but of dictatorships; the atom bomb, however, will force us more and more to imitate that absorption in military readiness so foreign to democracy, so natural for such a dictatorship as Soviet Russia.

There are those who feel that these grim consequences can be prevented, only if within the near future a well-developed form of world law and world government is put into effect. Little optimism for this course remains, as an early prospect, in view of the utter refusal of Russia to consider seriously the proposals agreed to by the rest of the world for a form of international administration designed to prevent the use of atomic discoveries for destructive purposes. On July 29, 1949 the United Nations Atomic Energy Commission, after three years barren of results, suspended their deliberations indefinitely.

Whether the grim prophecies of American democracy's corrosion will be confirmed depends upon a great many circumstances. Most of these are not directly related to atomic energy at all, and some of these I have endeavored to discuss in this book. One of the factors, however, that will clearly influence the outcome is the degree of perspective and sense of balance with which the American people and their leaders and representatives view these majestic discoveries.

That kind of perspective is not easily come by. We have a long way to go before attaining it. Far from a balanced view, we are still afflicted by the Myth of the Atom Bomb. The prospects for the future of democracy, in the sense in which I have been discussing that matter, seems to me adversely affected by this Myth.

The Myth is simply this: Atomic energy is useful only as a bomb, a weapon, and is actually nothing else.

If the Myth that atomic energy is simply a military weapon becomes a fixed thing in our minds, if we accept the error that it can never be anything else, we will never make it anything but a weapon. If we will drift into the belief, which so many appear already to hold, that all we need for our nation to be secure in a troubled world is this powerful weapon, we will tend to relax, when we should be eternally vigilant and alert.

The Myth will cause us to fall into an even deeper pit of error. We will grow forgetful of the true sources of a democracy's vitality and the true sources of our nation's strength. We will be misled into believing that America is strong because of military force alone, when in truth the foundation of our strength and amazing vitality is not in material things but rather in the spirit of this nation, in the faiths we cherish.

We are a people with a faith in each other, and when we lose that faith we are weak, however heavily armed. We are a people with a faith in reason, and the unending pursuit of new knowledge; and when we lose that faith we are insecure, though we be ever so heavily armed. We are a people with a faith in God, with a deep sense of stewardship to our Creator, the Father of us all; and when that is no longer strong within us we are weak and we are lost, however heavily armed with weapons—even with atomic weapons—we may be.

Nothing good ever comes from running away from reality; I am not urging that we put on a set of blinders so we will not see the dark and somber facts. But we must not become so preoccupied solely with the destructiveness of atomic energy that we think of its majestic discovery as a force of destruction and nothing else.

Our physical safety, our peace of mind, our clarity of thinking, and the conservation and strengthening of our faith in individual freedom require that all of us try to develop, rather promptly, a greater sense of balance about atomic energy. An important element in that better perspective we must seek is a fuller understanding that atomic energy discoveries, like life itself, have their dark and somber side, and also have their bright and hopeful side. Atomic energy bears that same duality that has faced man from time immemorial, a duality expressed in the Book of Books thousands of years ago: "See, I have set

before thee this day life and good and death and evil . . .
therefore choose life . . ."

Tens of thousands of men and women are today engaged upon pioneering forays into the atomic unknown.
They work with strange elements, new to man, as well as
with the commonplaces of concrete and lead. Some work
with no other equipment than their trained imagination
and a blackboard, others with some of the most complex
and ponderous mechanisms of all time. It is the brighter,
the more hopeful and beneficial actualities and promises
of our unfolding knowledge that occupy the time and
effort of a large segment of these thousands of men and
women who make up the atomic energy enterprise of this
country.

Atomic energy is a force as fundamental to life as the
force of the sun, the force of gravity, the forces of magnetism. It is an unfolding of new knowledge that goes to
the very heart of all physical things. Perhaps the greatest
single opportunity for new fundamental knowledge
about the nature of the physical world lies in the development of atomic energy. Within the atomic nucleus are
those deep forces, so terribly destructive if used for warfare, so beneficent if used to search out the cause and
cure of disease, so almost magical in their ability to pierce
the veil of life's secrets.

In the widening knowledge of the atom we have the
means for making our time one of the two or three most
vital, most intense and stimulating periods of all history.
In the atomic adventure we sight one of those great
mountain peaks of history, a towering symbol of one of

the faiths that makes man civilized, the faith in knowledge. I look forward to atomic development not simply as a search for new energy, but more significantly as a beginning of a period of human history in which this faith in knowledge can vitalize man's whole life.

Developments in the nucleus of the atom can by their force and example and stimulus spread to advances in all fields of knowledge. Indeed, by the contagion of achievement these advances may appear quite outside the physical sciences, in skills of statesmanship and human relations, and in the development of imagination and the spirit. In times like this, men rise above the plains of history.

Our chance for great adventure can however be lost to us. If this feeling of living in a very fruitful and special period is not sensed by people generally, and by our representatives and civic leaders, the atomic adventure may be stifled in the throes of politics, of routine, of sluggishness and apathy. The daring and style that pushed back other American frontiers will be missing.

There is evidence now and then that the shock and excitement of the Hiroshima blast has induced a kind of atomic neurosis, a constricting fear and hysteria that if allowed to continue and grow can distort our understanding of the true scope and meaning of the atomic development. We may, moreover, become momentarily so excited about sensations—such as the unfounded notion, for example, that automobiles can some day run on atomic energy pills—that this would exhaust our interest, and thereby we might miss the grand significance of the atomic prospect. Or, we might, because of false perspective become so preoccupied with pinchpenny economies as to lose sight of the opportunities for vast make-wealth creative efforts.

Only a great people, a people alive to the meaning of what is happening in our own time, can make this a great adventure. We are such a people.

Until quite recently man knew of only three kinds of forces: gravitational forces, which hold the universe together; electrical forces; and magnetic forces. The fourth, the newest to be even dimly understood—the one about which scientists still know next to nothing—are the nuclear forces in the atom: the infinitesimal building stones of which everything about us, all substances alive or inanimate, is constituted. A desk, the walls of a building, the mountains and the seas, are all composed of atoms and their nuclei.

No one can predict just what changes will come of this knowledge. Light is being thrown upon the very nature of the structure of the world we live in. This force is everywhere. Nothing is more pervasive, yet knowledge of it goes back only a few years. In the lifetime of men of my generation there has been discovered virtually all that is firmly known of the fourth major force.

For the citizens of the world's leading democracy to be in the dark as to the nature of the fundamental structure and forces of the atom—and of the great good as well as evil this knowledge can bring—would be for them to live in a world in which they are, in elementary knowledge, quite blind and unseeing. It would be almost as if they did not know that fire is hot, that water is wet; as if they did not know there are seasons and gravity and magnetism and electricity.

Nothing quite like the effect of this sudden knowledge upon the human mind has happened before in the case of a new idea or discovery; certainly not on such a scale. No wonder its possible effect on the future of democratic life and institutions is difficult to overstate.

In the past other great changes have taken place and have not been well understood at the time; most of them have not even been widely known. The voyage of Columbus marked a sharp turn in events, affecting every human life from that time forward, but apparently even Columbus himself did not understand what he had found. What people thought about the discovery of fire, the invention of the wheel, of gunpowder, of steam as a source of energy, of Faraday's discovery of electromagnetic induction (or electricity, as we say), of the discovery by Hertz of radio wave propagation at the time was certainly little, and what they did think was largely wrong.

Usually we have had a generation or even a century or two to adjust ourselves to the new and incomprehensible. This jump has been the biggest one we have ever been called upon to make in our thinking. After fifty years of continuous development the destructive power of chemical explosives was about doubled; the first atomic or nuclear explosive multiplied the power of the highest explosive previously known not by two times but by many millions of times—and this occurred virtually overnight. In the atomic furnace at Oak Ridge the energy being released from the splitting of the fissionable atoms of a pound of uranium is greater than that from the burning of a pound of coal by tens of millions of times. It is almost as if the Wright brothers in their first attempt at Kitty Hawk had flown several times around the world, or as if Marconi instead of tinkering with a spark gap started off with a coast-to-coast television network.

The development of atomic energy will pose many broad issues where the judgment of individual citizens will be essential, if they are to have a share in determining their democratic destiny. These include such matters as proposals for international control of atomic weapons; the conditions under which the present government monopoly in this field can safely be changed to private competitive production; the share of the national budget that should be devoted to scientific research; the adequacy of protection against health hazards from radioactive materials in the air and on the ground; the proper relation of civilian direction to the military in this field; what we need by way of navy, army, and air forces in the light of developments in scientific warfare; what sense the proposals make that we build our cities underground; the workability of decentralization of cities as a defense measure; how rapidly atomic fuel may supplement coal, oil, and water power as a source of electricity; the wisdom and workability of censorship of the press and radio as a means of maintaining secrecy in this field, under peacetime conditions. Such a list of policy issues could be extended almost indefinitely.

As if the problems of comprehension were not already

difficult enough this discovery comes at a time of world-wide bitterness and of international distrust such as has rarely existed before in time of peace.

We have been told that we must have world government and have it at once—within a definite and implacable time schedule of a few years—or we are goners. Our own special vulnerability to atomic warfare is told and retold in a way that is fearsome in the extreme. Maps of New York City are produced that show in detail just what ghastly horrors would occur if an atomic bomb no more powerful than those already used was dropped in the Hudson River or at Forty-second Street and Fifth Avenue. These accounts are technically correct, but harrowing. We were reminded that these bombs need not be dropped by air armadas that might be intercepted, but might conceivably be smuggled in, in parts, or concealed in the cargo of a tramp steamer moving innocently up the Hudson or into the Golden Gate.

Anyone at all experienced in human affairs recognizes fear as a dangerous state of mind. To those who have given little thought to such matters, it might have seemed a good idea to scare the world into being good, or at least sensible. But fear is brother to panic. Fear is an unreliable ally; it can never be depended upon to produce good. One result of intense fear may be panic, but another is likely to be phantasy, a dream-world. For men can stand great fear only so long. The sturdier ones look around for something specific they can do to overcome the cause of their fear. But most people unable long to endure fear turn to unreality. Things that are disturbing just don't exist. Other more pleasant objects are substituted. People who insist upon talking about unpleasant facts, and after awhile facts of any kind, are condemned or avoided.

If not fear, then what? A democracy's answer is: Understanding, comprehension, knowledge, perspective.

To meet the obvious difficulties of so large an order we have today some offsetting advantages. Never before in man's whole history did we have at hand such magic to aid in the communication of ideas and of information: the radio and television; our newspapers, magazines, and book publishers, now at a level of quality, usefulness and reliability unequaled in our history; the motion pictures with their infinite potentialities; our amazing network of educational agencies—schools in every hamlet, colleges and universities by the thousands, with the greatest enrollment of men and women in higher education ever known; the churches, and lay churchmen's organizations; the thousands of local societies and service clubs and Forums and libraries in every town and city. These are powerful forces for stimulating understanding and a sense of balance.

We shall need good steady judgment and cool heads in the coming years. In a democracy public thinking that is dominated by great fear, by phantasy, or by indifference to one of the central facts of our century provides a sorry foundation for the strains we may find it necessary to withstand, the hard decisions we must make, and the opportunities for a peaceful world that may be ours to develop.

What is in people's minds today about atomic energy is important in judging whether democracy will be stronger or weaker because of it. But of even greater importance is what may be in their minds next year at this time, or two or three years hence, when tensions may have increased, and when proposals may be made to jettison our practices of freedom, because of supposed necessities forced on us by the atom.

What may be in people's minds a year or two hence depends in part on leadership in each community and upon how successful the press, the radio and education generally will be in inspiring people to think clearly about and to appreciate the force of the facts about atomic energy.

A vacuum of knowledge about the atom will be filled; of that we may be sure. As time goes on it may be filled by utter indifference. This would be tragic and even disastrous for a people who will hear much easy talk about peace being had if we but wish for it hard enough. Such a vacuum of lack of knowledge may be filled by deep unreasoning fear and panic, or by phantasy, and illusions. Neither panic nor phantasy provides the basis for a world of peace and security.

But whether the vacuum is filled by indifference, or panic or wishful nonsense—the vacuum of public knowledge will be filled.

If people have knowledge and understanding our democratic precepts will be less subject to needless impairment, at our own hands. The peace of the world will be more secure. We will be less likely to be taken in by sweet talk, or scared by shadows, or stumble—or be pushed—without knowing what we are doing, into some desperate finality.

An informed democracy will take the facts as they come. It will set out to live with the facts, begin to take them into our thinking, into our everyday vocabulary.

We will then begin to form common sense judgments, not only as individuals, but as neighborhoods, as communities, as a people.

There is not a single one of us who is a mere spectator, who can turn a knob and tune himself out, or leave if he is bored, or horrified, or is more interested in his private affairs. We are all participants in that future chain of events that these epochal discoveries have set off. There are no supermen to solve these problems for us.

13. AN INFORMED PUBLIC MAY CONTROL ITS OWN DESTINY

An Informed Public
May Control Its Own Destiny

THIS is a time when we need especially to review how fundamental is public knowledge and public participation in determining our course as a democracy, and our security as a nation. There is no force, however powerful, however firmly entrenched, which can withstand united public opinion.

The core and the essence of democracy is the active participation of the people in governmental affairs. The atom has not changed this proposition. It has indeed heightened its importance. When the people do not participate, when they are uninformed or uninterested, when they cannot or will not make their voices heard or felt, when in short they default, the spirit of democratic action will soon die, and, indeed, if all this has occurred, already is on its way to extinction. But when the people individually and through their institutions and organizations are active watchmen and participants in the governmental activities of their communities and region and nation, then we have that fertile soil in which democracy flourishes and grows in strength and in fruitfulness.

This democracy of ours is founded upon a faith in the

over-all judgment and good sense of the people as a whole. Note that I am not speaking of "majorities," but of "the people as a whole." The magic lies not in the literal arithmetic of majority vote, but in the people's oft-proven sense of what is right and what is fair, that "sense of the meeting" that has at times so profoundly affected the course of American life.

We believe that when the people are honestly and clearly informed their conscience and their common sense can be relied upon to carry the nation safely through any crisis. This is not only our faith; by and large it is the actual practice of our American way of life.

This is not merely a kind of mysticism. As a matter of fact it is a rather hardheaded doctrine. Our experience has taught us that many heads are better than one head, many leaders better than one Leader. We believe in the process of practical testing. We put great store on discussion, on debate, on "chewing things over," on trying to "get the bugs out" of plans by skeptically examining them and probing them.

On every hand, these days, there is a ceaseless effort to persuade us of this and of that. We face an unending barrage of words and arguments and appeals. All of us are exposed to this effort from the time we (or our children) turn on our radio in the early morning. We are exposed to it through the newspaper, the magazine, the billboard, the television, the lecture and forum, the speech by the office-seeker. Someone is always trying to get our ear—and our approval: a salesman at the store,

a neighbor over a coke at the drugstore, the advocate of
the labor union or of organized agriculture, or those who
urge better highways, or greater or less military prepara-
tions, or more government intervention for you (and less
for them). On and on the many voices beat on our ears.

Someone is always at work trying, as the phrase goes,
"to sell the public." What we are being offered and what
we try to sell are ideas (or emotions). We hope these ideas
will persuade or move others to do or not to do, to
believe or not believe.

In international affairs, at a stormy time in the world,
the process of trying to "sell" ideas has taken the center
of the stage. It has become comparable in importance to
the methods of diplomacy. There are even those who
believe this method has made warfare in the conven-
tional sense obsolete. They argue that wars have become
an investment in bankruptcy for the victors; that a
cheaper and more effective way to extend a nation's influence is through "selling," that is to say, through influ-
encing the minds and emotions of men rather than
destroying their cities and then as "victors" supporting
them while they try to live on the battered and radioactive remnants.

How are we going to find our way amid all these voices,
all "selling" some idea? How can we sort out these appeals, identify falseness, baseness, recognize truth, reject
this and accept that, refine and distinguish and winnow
out the good from the bad? A great deal more than buying the wrong kind of washing machine will be the consequence of our being "sold" unsound ideas. Of this

there are tragic reminders as we see freedom lost in one nation after another.

The American people are quite willing to buy soap or toothpaste because somebody else recommends them and they are attractively advertised. But, thus far at least, they don't "buy" their economic or political opinions by such a process. As long as that is true we need not worry too greatly about the future of the Republic. As long as the American people make up their minds on important public questions, independently, by their own observations rather than by taking somebody else's word for it, as long as the Leader principle has no appeal, democracy is still in vigorous good health.

For this very reason to attain and to hold leadership in our American society it has always been necessary to appeal to the judgment of the people—the people in a community, in the case of local leadership and influence with one's neighbors; the people of the whole nation, in the case of a larger scene of activity. Neither hereditary claims, nor great wealth, nor well-deserved past glories guarantee continued leadership in American society. The place must be earned day by day. The test of leadership in America has been the ability to win the confidence not of a ruling class (for there is no such class) but the confidence and respect of the people as a whole.

We have long taken this phenomenon for granted. We grumbled at times because our neighbors were such idiots and had to be persuaded, rather than take the say-so of some Great Mind or other. But, unfortunately, frequently these Great Minds turned out to be wrong, so that we are now not often tempted to short-cut the slower, cruder, sometimes impolite system of hammering things out by public discussion, in the wholesome atmosphere of "you've-got-to-show-me."

It is against such a background of our faith in education—education in its broadest sense as a foundation stone of democracy—that Congress placed in the Atomic Energy Act of 1946 a quite remarkable "Declaration of Policy." This Declaration states:

The effect of the use of atomic energy for civilian purposes upon the social, economic, and political structures of today cannot now be determined. It is a field in which unknown factors are involved. *Therefore, any legislation will necessarily be subject to revision from time to time.* It is reasonable to anticipate, however, that tapping this new source of energy will cause profound changes in our present way of life. (My italics)

This is a statement almost unique among declarations by governments, for note that it insists, rather proudly in fact, that we do not now have all the answers. A dictator, or the head of a military-dominated nation, could hardly afford to make such an admission; the representatives of a free people can. Congress, reflecting a general mood, approached atomic energy in 1945 and 1946 with the attitude that as a people we can meet these problems and solve them only if we learn more. The frankness of this admission is evidence of our strong confidence in the democratic process even when confronted with a complex technical subject. It is evidence of our faith in the over-all judgment of the people, and of our reliance upon the processes and the techniques of education.

In our several tasks of self-education, we ought to start close to home. We should start with those things about us that we know and can wholly understand. Then our thinking can move outward to the broader reaches of national and world affairs. There is a human tendency to go in for tall talk and generalizations as broad as the horizon. It is no strain to stand around the cracker barrel or the soda fountain and solve world problems or the difficulties of some far-off country, China, say, or India or France. And to speculate vaguely and soulfully on "whither are we drifting" puts only a slight burden on the mind. But it is hard work to make specific plans about the problems of our own home town, our own business, our own region. That is tough and exacting—but it is the starting point, for the strength of America rests upon the strength of individuals, communities, and regions. What goes on in the homes and the communities all through America, and not alone what goes on in Washington or New York or Moscow or London or Berlin, will determine our fate.

The history of our time will be written by what happens in the everyday lives of the men and women we see upon the streets and in the factories and on the farms and in the colleges and city halls and the legislatures and the administrative offices and the business establishments of America. When we have that idea clearly in our minds we will, in my opinion, be far along the road in meeting and overcoming the threat to freedom in the world.

To say this does not lessen the tremendous import of

the broad issues of national policy and international policy, that we hear much discussed. I am only sure that citizens have a better opportunity to make their voices heard in the determination of those broad issues, if at the same time they are hard at work on the more specific problems that arise and must be largely determined within each community.

The demands upon an informed and responsible citizenship are constantly growing. Science and technical matters will become increasingly more important in determining peace and security. More and more things of daily life in the factory and school and farm will be affected by the discoveries and applications of science. This can be made pretty much to the good for peace and human freedom if we do not let these new technical advances get out of our power to control and direct in accordance with our democratic heritage.

What should concern us, it seems to me, is not that changes are coming. Americans have always taken change in their stride; indeed, generally speaking, we thrive on it. What we should make sure of is that the changes shall be fitted into the American way of doing things, and not be so imposed upon us that individual freedom is impaired. We must make sure that the American people will have a decisive say-so in the adjustments these discoveries will bring in community life, in our agricultural, educational, industrial and military institutions.

The people, however, can be barred from a decisive voice, by their own default, if they fail to become reasonably well informed. The necessity for knowledge is not to satisfy mere curiosity nor in this instance to develop "culture." The purpose should be to enable the people to participate in decisions of the greatest moment to themselves, to their businesses and homes, to the perpetuity of their institutions, and to their freedom and that of their children.

In issues turning upon scientific or engineering matters what is needed is not detailed knowledge and technical judgment but enough factual information on which to base judgments on policy issues. What is needed even more than technical knowledge are such qualities as good sense about human relations and standards of fairness, and what things people will accept as right and workable. These judgments often turn on the weight that ought to be given to concern for the individual as compared to concern for "the state." The issues call for the kind of over-all judgment that is summed up when your neighbor says: "That makes sense to me." There has never been nor can there be any good substitute for the all-around common sense of an informed public.

The whole fabric of international relations has been affected by the discoveries concerning atomic energy. The nature of war and therefore the ways in which wars are fought, and prevented and begun, has been profoundly affected. Atomic energy raises broad questions that go to the heart of the constitutional position of the President, questions about secrecy in a democracy, secrecy in scientific research, and about the role of Congress in the supervision of a technical enterprise.

In this country we are engaged with a program to create an atomic energy enterprise so large, so well staffed and managed, aided by such great industries and universities, that the United States of America will not only continue to lead but will establish an unquestionable and unchallenged superiority not only in weapons but in basic science, agriculture, industry, power, nutrition and in all the other fields which this new area of knowledge touches. Hence as citizens I urge that we become informed about broad areas of facts about atomic energy, areas that are not secret in any way.

I mention atomic energy particularly, but only as an example. True, it is an urgent and critical example, but nevertheless only one of many equally appropriate to this chapter's theme. The European Recovery Program—the Marshall Plan—provides another appropriate example. Here too the determination of the broad policy issues and the way, broadly speaking, in which the program is carried out, affect every one of us. These policies need to be analyzed and discussed with the help of a fund of ever-increasing knowledge, so the time-tested good sense and good will of the American people can make itself felt at every stage of this huge undertaking in peace and reconstruction. Other examples are the proposals for the development of the basic natural resources of this country, such as those for a Columbia Valley and a Missouri Valley Administration.

It is important that the needed facts and the analyses of policies should come from a variety of sources, not from only a few. This variety gives every citizen a chance to check one version against another, and draw his own conclusions. The press, the radio, the various kinds of periodicals, are competent to take the body of knowledge that exists and with their great skills of presentation make any subject reasonably clear and alive for every school child, and every grown-up in America. The colleges and the schools can assemble and boil down the relevant facts about public issues for the use of local civic organizations.

Such help as this from the outside is necessary, and can be very useful, when it comes to an analysis and a discussion of these things. But people should not be content to take ideas just as they have been predigested for them at some distant place. The programs of lay church groups, of the local Chamber of Commerce, the local Boy Scouts and Girl Scouts, the unions, the Parent-Teachers Association, Rotary, Kiwanis, Lions and similar organizations, the League of Women Voters, the 4-H Clubs, the County Farm Bureau or Grange or Farmers Union, the local veterans organizations, the business and professional women's organization, the bar association and county medical society can bring information and different points of view.

The American people, talking these things over in all the neighborhoods of this broad land, can get an understanding of the essentials of the new forces active in the world of today that may make the difference between calamity and progress. For the Great Consensus, the conscience and the judgment of the people as a whole, is one of the sturdiest pillars of democracy.

14. LABOR AND MANAGE-
MENT CAN WORK TO-
GETHER: AN EXAMPLE,
A CHALLENGE

Labor and Management
Can Work Together:
An Example, A Challenge

O NE of the most persuasive and appealing demonstrations of the superiority of democratic principles
is our remarkable success in making the processes of collective bargaining work effectively, and in increasing the
workers' opportunity to promote good management and
profitable operation of the industries in which they earn
their living. Indeed, it is not too much to say that the
health and strength of American democracy depend to a
large degree upon the continued improvement and development of relations between free and uncoerced organizations of labor, and free and uncoerced industrial
management.

It is true, of course, that we have our "labor problems." From time to time they are serious, even critical.
When, however, one considers in perspective the movement of events of the past quarter century he will not,
I believe, find in any like period of history any comparable area of human affairs wherein the essentials of freedom and the increased importance of the individual have
been so greatly strengthened.

This successful demonstration of voluntary methods in contrast with the methods of legal enforcement and of dictation is fundamental to the whole issue of the preservation and extension of democracy. In making these observations about industrial labor relations I do not at the moment refer to the importance to democracy of high levels of production at ever lower costs, or that in a democracy we risk everything if we habitually become embroiled in bitter class conflicts. I am thinking of something that goes even deeper.

One can, it seems to me, judge whether an institution of human affairs such as American labor-management relations adds to the strength of democracy, or weakens and corrodes it, by answering three questions about that institution. Does it encourage and stimulate the release of the creativeness, the energies, and the potentialities of individual human beings? Does it diminish the arbitrary power of one man over other men? Does it increase the sense of individual responsibility for work carried on by a group of individuals?

As applied to labor relations in the United States today, and looking at the picture as a whole, the answer to all three of these test questions, it seems to me, should be in the affirmative; therefore this human institution deserves to be judged a source of added vitality to democracy.

During the past twenty-five years I have had an opportunity to observe these matters from both the labor union and the management side of the table. It seems to me clear that very substantial progress, in democratic human terms, has been made. I see no decisive reason why we cannot continue this forward development of our system of free labor and free management. From such growth and refinement we can receive greater and greater strength for our kind of society, in terms of the release of individual human energies and potentialities, in the decrease of arbitrary power, and the increase of a sense of individual responsibility.

This country has had a democratic form of government for more than one hundred and fifty years. We are now in the process of applying the principles of democracy to our industrial activity which we have so long applied to our civic institutions.

We have set up high goals for this country. We have attained a very high level of income for our whole people; we seek to keep income, production and employment at relatively high levels. War production has shown what prodigious things can be accomplished. To succeed, to the full, I believe our plans and programs must include the creative and productive potentialities of trained and skillful workers, of responsible and constructive management and the will to establish and use modern methods of securing cooperation through responsible labor-management relations.

Such a system of union-management relations needs to be seen as an asset, not as a necessary nuisance. It cannot be thought of simply as a truce between two natural enemies. Union-management cooperation is a tool whereby American enterprise can increase its vigor, its creativeness, and chief of all its part in developing individual freedom and well-being. Labor needs to feel that it "belongs." By this I mean that labor understand, by the attitude not only of its employer but, even more, of the whole community, that its special talents and skills and judgment are desired and prized.

The A. F. of L. publication *The Federationist* for August, 1924, uses these words:

> To include the union among the functional divisions of the industry removes a cause of incalculable industry waste. . . . To accord to the union opportunity to perform its constructive function means linking another power group into a coordinated system. Each worker is a power unit contributing both physical and brain power. . . . Each human power unit may be working automatically and unthinkingly or each may alertly use tools, machinery and materials, vigilantly watching each development with that creative attitude of mind that assures progress. The union is essential to maintaining this quality of workmanship. The union makes these individual power sources a coordinated, directed power undertaking, assures the worker his rights and makes it possible for him to concentrate on his duties. The union coordinates individual capacities into a power pool.

TVA is this kind of a coordinated "power pool," a pooling of the abilities of thousands of workers and supervisors working on a job they believe in, a job to which they give their best. One of the largest construction jobs ever undertaken either by government or private business, and the country's largest coordinated power system, it is being run the way I believe most

American citizens would like to have such a job run, and the way most of the leaders and the rank and file of workmen want the job done.

When TVA began its first construction work the law gave the Board of Directors a real choice of how to carry out the job. It could be delegated to contractors, the almost invariable practice in government construction. Or it could be undertaken directly by employees of the TVA. We decided that, with minor exceptions, the job would be done by "force account" and not by contract, that is, by the direct employment of the workers by TVA. This was entirely workable, for Congress had set up TVA, not as a government bureau, bound in endless red tape, but as a corporation, deliberately granted by law the flexibility and capacity for initiative of a private enterprise. Operating by "force account" meant that the direct and full responsibility for labor policy, for hours, rates of pay, working conditions, and the adjustment of disputes rested squarely on the TVA. These conditions obtain today.

This was a pioneer undertaking, a new kind of job. TVA believed its policies and practices might set a precedent and standard for labor policies in the United States Government and to some extent for private industry. Those labor policies ought to be right. They ought to conform to good public policy and the best traditions of the labor movement.

We realized that if TVA failed to establish fair and workable relations between the human beings working on that job, the whole project would probably be a failure, even if every physical objective were reached. What permanent good will it do our country to save our soil, to control floods, and to distribute cheap electricity if those goals are reached with disregard for the individual worker, or by methods that cast aside the desire of labor to have a creative role in such an undertaking? That would be not progress but a step backward. It is not too much to say that unless TVA's labor policy is just, the whole regional program is out of step with democracy.

We believed that the important thing in business management is not the wage rate per hour, but the total cost to get a certain amount of work done. When men are paid reasonable wages; when they are led by their foremen and not driven; when they have protection against arbitrary power and unfairness; when they have decent hours and conditions; when they believe in what they are doing, they do better work and usually at less cost per unit. We believed it was the job of the supervisory staff to exert itself to cut costs by better methods of management, rather than taking it out of the hide of labor.

The basic policy as to wages was determined by the Congress, which required that prevailing wages should be paid, and that in determining the prevailing wages due consideration should be given to those arrived at by the voluntary methods of collective bargaining. This in itself is an important determination of democratic policy.

Those in charge of this project on behalf of our stockholders, the people of the United States, believed that labor should have an opportunity to participate actively in management problems, and that organized labor by and large was willing and able to make a notable contribution to these management policies.

One of the great difficulties in relations between management and workmen in large enterprises has been that management has so largely lost contact with the human beings who really make things go. This is by no means a matter of choice. In the huge private corporations and the enormous government agencies of these times, it takes a special effort on the part of management and supervisors to maintain this human contact, to know what the men working under their direction think and how they feel about things. No amount of skill in administration and no perfection of organization can take the place of the kind of human understanding that comes from keeping in touch on a man-to-man basis. No matter how smart we may be about machines and how big and powerful we may design and build them, behind every piece of machinery is a human being. Machines will go as long as they are fed their fuel and maintained physically, but human beings fortunately are different. Men and women do not work for bread alone, and any industrial leader, or labor leader, or public leader, who forgets that is in for trouble.

The TVA labor policy was not laid down on the barrel-head, "take-it-or-leave-it." It was the outgrowth of genuine democracy as applied to labor relations on a huge construction job. All the way up and down the Valley, representatives of labor and of management met together and worked out the principles to govern on this job, embodied in an "Employee Relationship Policy." A newspaper man described it in this way:

Well-versed students of industrial problems regard the far-reaching agreement, which represents a model for Government and private industry, as remarkable not only for its text and the brief time in which it was negotiated, but also for the fact that no acts of strife accompanied its writing.

This novel pact of men and management was not written in blood on the traditional field of industrial warfare, nor was it handed down from on high and meekly accepted by the employees as the best they could hope for without an agonizing struggle. It was, instead, the product of true collective bargaining. . . .

In 22 short paragraphs the "Employee Relationship Policy" resolved conflicts that have cost many lives, countless millions in property and untold suffering in the industrial world.

This policy provides first of all for collective bargaining. Collective bargaining is a reality on the TVA job. It is being practiced honestly and effectively, and the results have paid off for labor, for management, and for the stockholders, who are the American people.

The TVA labor policy recognizes the right of employees to organize and, in the exercise of this right, assures them that they shall be free from any and all restraint, interference, or coercion on the part of the management and supervisory staff. Channels are established so that an employee, through his representative, can present his claim or grievance in an orderly way. He can be assured of a fair review, not only by his immediate superiors but, if he is not satisfied, by a properly constituted appeal authority as well. The door is wide open for him and his associates to bring their difficulties, criticism, or suggestions to the attention of the management as a normal, legitimate expression of the employee's interest in the job.

When TVA is discussing major policies and rules and regulations affecting rates of pay, hours, and working conditions, the local and international representatives are invited to sit in. As an illustration of this, the Personnel Division of TVA, which the Board of Directors holds responsible for interpreting and administering its labor policy, held its first annual conference three months after the labor policy had been adopted. To this conference were invited the business agents and representatives of the unions who, day after day, are in touch with their members on the job. This conference threshed out problems which were coming to light in the application and administration of the policy labor had helped management to formulate.

It is sound policy for a governmental corporation such as TVA to remove obstructions in the way of the self-organization of its working forces. This is more than a matter of efficiency in carrying on a construction and operating project, although I am convinced that it is the most efficient way of doing it; it is more than a matter of recognizing responsibility to human beings on the part of the Government. This policy goes beyond these

things. Organization—effective, responsible, bona fide
organization of wage earners—aids in the preservation of
all democratic institutions.

The TVA has met its responsibility, and, in its part of
the bargain, labor has met its part of the responsibility.
The so-called "local joint cooperative committees" will
illustrate the point. In the first place, whether such a joint
committee of labor and management shall be organized
at all, at a particular location, is a matter for labor-
management consultation and agreement. The regular
monthly meeting of the joint cooperative committee of
TVA's ammonium nitrate production plant at Muscle
Shoals on July 20, 1948 indicates the way these committees function. Six representatives of labor were
present and five from local management. Each labor
member reported on particular suggestions they had
made to improve operations. The proposals covered a
wide area: among them, an automatic device on dump
grates in all boilers, a relief valve for bleeding excess low
pressure steam to atmosphere, a shed over the coal un-
loading hopper at the steam plant. On this last proposal
the worker submitted preliminary drawings of his idea
that he had worked out at home. One man suggested a
better method of repairing the base of towers used in the
chemical process.

This particular meeting was attended by a consultant
for the Congressional Joint Committee on Labor
Management Relations. In the Report of that Committee (May 12, 1949) prepared by Mr. Alexander K.
Christie, are these observations on this meeting:

There was nothing haphazard about the suggestions put forth. They were thoroughly discussed by both representatives of labor and management and if the suggestion was shown to be impractical, it was voted down, only after exhausting all possibilities. . . . Where the available evidence was not complete, the workman responsible for the suggestion was advised by the members of the conference to gather more facts . . . and present them at the next meeting. . . . It is suggestions such as these that have made the operation of these plants more and more efficient and have continued to boost production, while operating costs have decreased. . . . The promotion of cooperation between labor and management has worked out to the benefit of both. The employees of TVA have become more aware of the problems facing management. TVA . . . has greatly benefited from the cooperation and greater interest in the job by the employee.

Another illustrative instance: The job committee of one of the carpenters' locals noticed that on one of the dam construction jobs used lumber was not being salvaged as economically as the committee thought it ought to be. It drew up a plan for wrecking concrete forms by using apprentices and laborers; this would make it possible to save thousands of feet of lumber. Management might have caught this item, of course; but labor saw it first and helped save this material for the TVA. The local committee made the suggestion because it wanted to save TVA money, the taxpayer's money, not to put management "on the spot." These men thought of themselves as partners in the enterprise.

The training of men in higher skills and in new skills is a field in which, without organized labor's participation and leadership, both industry and educational institutions are not only handicapped but almost frustrated.

TVA and labor have jointly set the standards of skill and efficiency of workers on TVA projects; together they have trained men and women for many kinds of work. Joint Labor-Management Committees cooperating with schools have in all, trained thousands of craft apprentices, power plant operators, and industrial workers in the manufacture of chemicals and fertilizers. The Joint Committees have outlined the skills to be mastered, the related courses to be taken. The Joint Committees have established supplementary requirements of a knowledge of regional development.

The result is far more than an efficient labor supply for TVA. This cooperation has produced a standard of skill and workmanship, and has contributed directly to the process of production and regional development. As important as anything, it has also enriched the lives of individuals.

In the TVA job organized labor has done more than bargain collectively for its wages and working conditions, present grievance cases, and render a day's work for a day's wage. Organized labor has put its heart and its spirit and its good will into the TVA's job. Whenever that happens in industrial operations or in public enterprises then you really see the blossoming of great things. The workman and strawboss and foreman and member of the executive staff knows that he has a responsibility for making the project a success, for keeping down costs, for devising better methods of doing the job. The men on that job act as if in the eyes of the American people the success or failure of the job depends on them. Which it does. As a result, there is an enthusiasm and loyalty not to the boss but to a goal larger than any one man. This gives a spirit to the job without which the project would have far less meaning.

The entire panorama of a region's life and development is the appropriate and the wise scope of labor's interest and of labor's participation in such a regional program as TVA. Labor's chief interest, as is that of all citizens and all groups of citizens, should be in everything that goes to make up a strong nation—the prosperity of farmers and of businessmen, flourishing industry, soil fertility, flood control, the vitalization of schools and universities. Labor's interest is far broader than a special and wholly legitimate interest in its own wages, hours, and working conditions.

I well recall an all-day conference between the TVA Board and staff and a group from organized labor, at which no reference to wages or conditions of employment were mentioned or discussed. Such meetings are for an exchange of views about the development of natural resources in the Valley, and the place that development has in strengthening the economic underpinning of the whole South.

Labor has often expressed a lively interest in the agricultural program of the Valley. Since most of the labor representatives were born or brought up on farms they could easily understand that if the soil of the Tennessee Valley was lacking in fertility, that if erosion was carrying that soil off the land and into the streams, not only would the farmers be poorer, and the Valley poorer, but labor would be poorer. Industrial workers would be worse off because an impoverished agriculture would throw a surplus of labor into industry at the same time that farmers could not absorb the products of industrial plants. When freight rate discrimination against the South was a lively topic of discussion labor saw clearly how great a stake their membership has in anything that is an unjust restrictive burden upon the region's industry and business.

The leaders of organized labor, from the information they gain in their working partnership with the TVA, carry a good deal back with them into the daily stream of life and affairs throughout the Valley. These leaders, the members of the Tennessee Valley Trades and Labor Council, are active, responsible citizens in their home communities. As men leave TVA jobs for private employment, many take with them not only new skills but broader understanding.

The splitting of the atom has created a new industry. The problems of developing creative labor-management relations in this field are as unique as they are puzzling; they are in striking contrast to those encountered in the TVA regional program, and to those in private industry generally.

The objective, of course, is the same: to make increasingly democratic in principle and in practice the relations of individual workers to those responsible for management through the voluntary processes of collective bargaining and labor-management cooperation. But clearly this is a severe test of the flexibility and universality of our principles. However, a beginning has been made since October 1948, when the Atomic Energy Commission stated to unions and industrial contractors "that there is a place for and a need for organized labor in the atomic energy program." In September 1948 the ban on unions of operating employees that existed during the war was lifted by the Commission. But there is a long way to go before a thoroughly satisfactory adaptation — for that is what it must be—of industrial democracy and the best in American labor-management practice can be made to work out in this strange new industry.

For it is a strange business. It is surrounded by conditions quite different from our usual ways of doing things. It is a business in parts of which, day in and day out, the industrial materials are seen by the workmen only through a periscope, and are handled by remote control behind many feet of concrete or under many feet of liquid. At Oak Ridge, during the war it was necessary in one huge room to take infinite precautions against even the finest particle of dust getting into the air. In addition to many air filters and similar devices dozens of women kept pushing vacuum sweepers back and forth over a floor that was obviously spic and span. On the day after the bomb drop in Japan it was announced that Oak Ridge had been engaged in an atom-splitting project. People in the town went around asking their neighbors: "What did you do about splitting the atom?" One of the vacuum sweeper women, her puzzlement over at last, said with pride: "I was a-sweepin' up them atom husks."

But even stranger things than sweeping up atom husks make the development of democratic industrial relations a tough problem here. The clear necessity of secrecy, in wide areas of an industry, is one example. The requirements are made more difficult by the fact that they must be maintained in the face of all our peacetime habits and inclinations and at a time when the existence of the project is no longer secret.

There are many other factors that add to the difficulties of this adjustment: These industrial plants are owned by the Government but operation is delegated by the Commission to many private concerns, each with its own ideas about labor unions and conditions of work; the extreme security precautions that are taken (including the use of the polygraph or lie detector) to account for the last fraction of an ounce of metals that workmen fabricate and handle in quantities of thousands and thousands of tons; the necessity for full investigation by the Federal Bureau of Investigation of all workers, and local and sometimes even national union officers, and their security clearance by the Commission, introduces into an already difficult situation a factor that not only can cause irritation and even resentment by workers, but one that must be constantly watched lest it be abused and used as a means of discrimination or of interference with normal union activities; and finally the absolute technical requirement that certain huge industrial operations may not stop even for a split second, much less for a day or a month's strike or lockout.

This will surely make evident some of the difficulties in the way of genuinely democratic labor-management relations. The difficulties are great; so also is the need, for in this industry one must have the very best of energies and good will of the individual workers. Where interruption of operation is quite literally unthinkable in a physical sense, as is true in a number of important operations, and where urgency is the keynote, industrial cooperation takes on a heightened importance. There is irony in the fact that it is in the field of atomic energy (the newest and farthest advance of the machine age) that we find the human being and good human relations at their peak of importance.

In the TVA, that government corporation was the direct employer of the entire labor force. The Atomic Energy Commission's policy and practice however (as I have outlined in an earlier chapter) has been to engage industrial corporations to construct and to operate its plants. The policy appears to me to be sound, under the circumstances I have cited, but it clearly adds a serious complication to the development of labor relations. The Commission's industrial labor policies must, in the main, be made effective indirectly, through the Commission's industrial partners, rather than directly. It is true that while the wages of all employees, such as those of the

General Electric Company at the Hanford plant of the Commission, or those of the Carbide and Carbon Corporation at Oak Ridge, for example, are fully reimbursed to the companies by the Commission, it is our policy that these employees be considered as employees of General Electric or Carbide, not of AEC.

If the Commission (because it is ultimately responsible and because it foots the wage bill) itself decides all the tough questions of labor relations—recognition of unions, wages, benefit plans, and so on—then our efforts to increase the sense of responsibility and initiative on the part of General Electric and Carbide (and the other participating industries) are rendered nugatory; the industrial concern tends to become a mere automaton. As a consequence its incentive to develop and improve these relationships, according to its own ideas, would disappear. And yet, if as a result of poor labor-management standards and practices worker morale is low, antagonism between unions and management is chronic, and (in the extreme case) interruption or slowdowns occur, the increased costs, impaired efficiency, and physical disaster that might ensue are the responsibilities of the Commission. These are factors of difficulty not commonly found in a labor situation.

But the troubles only begin here. Add the element of secrecy and the protection of secret data and the safeguarding of atomic materials. Add, too, the fact that each industrial employee or anyone else who has access to secret information must be investigated by the FBI and cleared by the Commission. Out of all of this an atmosphere abnormal to American industry is created, and the strange—but necessary—conditions give rise to all manner of situations foreign to our democratic concepts, and a handicap to the development of the best labor-management relations.

A few examples will make this clear. It is fundamental that employees must be free to select their representatives without any interference from anyone, and particularly from the employer. But how can that principle be made to square with the following situation? The officers of a union representing the employees in a plant using secret processes are not employees in the plant; if they do not have access to secret information they have not been FBI-investigated as all employees must be who have such access. But such union officers might be able to use their official position and their influence with employees who are members of the union deliberately to hamper or shut down atomic production for reasons that are political (such as to carry out a disloyal "party line") rather than for reasons related to wages, hours, working conditions, or other valid union concerns. Where, therefore, in a rare case the records of union officers raise serious questions about their reliability, those questions must be disposed of satisfactorily. There has been one important case in which the officers refused even to discuss such questions; thereupon the Commission directed the employing industry to refuse to recognize that particular union. This meant that the government, in the interests of security, clearly departed from the normally accepted principle of not interfering in the selection by workers of their union officers.

The case I have last cited is clearly an unusual one. But even in the most routine of day-to-day operations the same abnormal situation is present. Thus, in an ordinary grievance case involving secret work, the union spokesman for the employee must be investigated by the FBI, and be approved by the Commission even before he may secure admittance to the plant. If the conditions of secret work in a plant are objected to by employees, before their union representatives (if non-employees) can go into the plant to investigate the complaint (or even, in fact, before the complaint can be described to them by the workers they represent), they must receive the appropriate security approval from the Commission. This security-test atmosphere permeates almost all labor-management relations. It is obvious that such abnormal, burdensome, and trying conditions increase manyfold the difficulties of securing and maintaining the highest standard of cooperation between labor and management in this new industry.

As things stand in the world today it certainly will take time and patient experimentation to find a way whereby the essential principles of labor-management can be adapted to the necessities and special circumstances that surround atomic energy. A long step in this direction was taken in April, 1949, in the Report to President Truman and to the Atomic Energy Commission, of a Presidential Commission on Labor Relations in the Atomic Energy Installations. The Commission was made up of Aaron

Horvitz, Edwin E. Witte, and William H. Davis, who was also its chairman.

In a report to Congress in January, 1948, the Atomic Energy Commission had summarized the aims of its labor relations policy in these words:

(a) Wholehearted acceptance by contractors and by labor and its representatives of the moral responsibility inherent in participation in the atomic energy program; (b) Development of procedures to assure (1) that all participants in the program are loyal to the United States, including those whose participation involves the exercise of negotiating and disciplinary authority over bargaining units, and (2) that determination of unit, jurisdiction, and similar questions will not breach security: (c) Continuity of production at vital AEC installations; (d) Consistent with the Commission's responsibility under the law, the least possible governmental interference with the efficient management expected from the AEC contractors; (e) Minimum interference with the traditional rights and privileges of American labor.

The Davis Commission, noting those objectives, recommended that management and labor voluntarily "forego all resort to strikes, lockouts and other interruptions of any such operations" until certain of its recommended procedures for the settlement of disputes had been fully pursued. The procedure called for the establishment by the Atomic Energy Commission of a Labor Relations Panel appointed by the President from nominations submitted to him by the Commission. This Panel was not to arbitrate, nor to mediate in every dispute, but to act in unusual situations only, where collective bargaining and all the normal processes of conciliation had clearly failed, and where as a consequence the continuity of an essential operation of the program was threatened.

The Commission adopted the recommendations of the Presidential panel; virtually all unions and employers in the program voluntarily agreed to abide by the terms calling for maintenance of the status quo.

This does not mean, however, that labor-management difficulties will not arise or strike votes may not be taken, or that strikes are an absolute impossibility. But it does mean that the temptation to substitute compulsory arbitration or government fiat for collective bargaining has been put aside, one may hope indefinitely.

Among the Davis Commission's recommendations are two that express my hope—more than hope, my confident expectation—that even in this unusual but crucial industry our democratic principles can be made effective. I quote the two passages below:

"That, subject to the Commission's responsibility under the law and to the limitations specified in other paragraphs of these recommendations, the normal and typical aspects of wages, hours, and working conditions which are the substance of collective bargaining between private employers and nongovernmental employees shall in Government-owned, privately operated atomic energy installations be left to collective bargaining between management and labor free from governmental interference.

That in all Government-owned, privately operated atomic

energy installations in which representatives have been chosen by the workers and lawfully designated, or recognized by management, management and union cooperate to integrate the union into the plant organization as a two-way channel of communication and a medium of understanding between management and workers.

15. TOWARD A GREATER AMERICA

Toward a Greater America

MANY years ago Walt Whitman used to wander along the Atlantic seaboard celebrating America in words that ring. He told his countrymen of the great strength and vigor and beauty of America. He sang of a stout and powerful land—strong, and bragging of its strength. Old Walt shouted to the universe that this was the greatest country ever heard of. That was true then; it is still true.

I wish Walt Whitman were alive today to continue his immortal song. We need badly to talk about what a wonderful land and people we are, for we suffer at times from a kind of national jitters.

We are sometimes told that we are torn with disunity and rife with disloyalty, that "the rich get richer and the poor get poorer." This is rubbish. We have weaknesses and they must be carefully assessed. We do have some who are not loyal and they need watching. But it is even more important to remember how strong and vital and how united we are, the voice of Walt Whitman supporting us, the voice that many years ago chanted these words:

Long, too long America.
Traveling roads all even and peaceful you learn'd from joys
    and prosperity only,

But now, ah now, to learn from crises of anguish, advancing,
    grappling with direct fate and recoiling not,
And now to conceive and show to the world what your
    children en-masse really are . . .

We can in very truth "show to the world" a nation that
is knitted firmly, for the regions of the United States, and
the people of this country, are drawing closer one to another. No tariff barriers, no separate languages, no deep
bitterness prevent that movement.

We shall survive as a free people, for the men and
women of America carry deep in their hearts a burning
conviction that the nation they have built is worth every
sacrifice they may be called upon to make. The stubborn
loyalty and devotion of the average American, I am
convinced, can carry us through every crisis, if we can
make it plain by actions that are so much more persuasive
than even the most eloquent words, that the troubles
and the aspirations of the average man and woman everywhere are matters of deep and lasting concern to our
leaders and rank and file alike. When the Nation's morale
is reared on such a foundation, there is in truth a defense
well-nigh impregnable.

Hope and pride and confidence in the hearts of men,
where before were frustration and despair is the rock
on which the defense of American democracy ultimately
rests.

It would be wholesome if we were to revive that good
old-fashioned custom of bragging about America. In
Whitman's time it was common enough to celebrate the

Nation, its area, its power, its opportunities, the character and spirit of its people. Then something happened. Our novels and our plays began to make fun of our boasting. The American traveler abroad who was always telling about what a great country this was became a standard joke. We stopped bragging and began to apologize for ourselves, for our Babbitts, for our failure to cultivate the arts and graces. We even became apologetic—or some Americans did—for being the strongest and most dramatically beautiful land on earth. No great national spirit can be built up by wearing a hair-shirt and sitting in the ashes of our shortcomings. In the period of prolonged tension and emergency we now must endure, such morbid faultfinding can sap our strength. The armament of a democracy must include pride and confidence.

I am not one who underestimates the prophylaxis of criticism. I know the danger of complacency, that we have our slums in city and country, our depressed areas, and many other things that are ugly and evil. We have the highest standard of living in the world, but we know it is unevenly distributed. We suffer from the paradox of plenty—too much wheat on the plains, but still not enough bread on the tables. But of this I am sure: If we spend our energies wailing and moaning and shaking in our boots, we shall find our courage badly depleted at the very time when we need to be confident, steady, and sure.

For myself, I am proud that we are by all odds the strongest industrial nation in the world. I have no apologies to make to anyone that we do things in a big way.

The song of America, however, is not only one of steel and oil and automobiles; not only one of material things. We have a solidarity and a unity of spirit and purpose that we can brag about. We can boast with truth that nowhere on the face of the earth in any period of human history has there been a vast nation less cursed with deep class divisions. Here there are no fixed classes as in Europe; no landed gentry, no bowing and scraping. If you call an American worker a member of the proletariat you may get a black eye for your pains. Nor has there ever been a vast nation in which the different national and racial groups have been so readily assimilated. The melting pot has really melted. That is something to brag about.

We have been through two decades of fluctuating economic conditions, sometimes of great unemployment and business failures, of war and conscription, of worry and despair for millions of people. Almost any other country might have experienced extensive violence and bloodshed, even civil war. We did not strain a seam of the Ship of State. We did not even approximate a revolt. The homes of the rich were not stormed; there were no heads on pikes. There was great suffering; there were a few cases of tragic violence. Here and there the militia was called out. But considering the real or fancied provocation to militant protest, that is perhaps the proudest record of social unity through times of stress in the history of any country, ancient or modern.

This is not the whole story. In America what is *right* matters to the average citizen, and the *truth* matters. A man's reputation among his fellows as a truthful and kindly human being means more in the long run than anything else. Compare this standard with that of the countries where there is now a premium on lying and deceit and brutality.

In the towns that I am familiar with in the South, or in the Middle West where I was "brought up," as one goes about his daily affairs, up and down the streets, he finds the kindliest, the friendliest, the straightest, the most independent people on earth today, in spite of all they have been through since 1929. Think of the students, of the young bank clerks, the filling station men, the airplane pilots, the man in the drugstore, the farmers on their tractors, the redcaps in the stations—if one runs his mind over the men and women he sees and talks to and does business with day after day—he finds there good will and decency; he finds the human qualities that can surmount any crisis the years of tension for the democracies may develop.

The genius of America is in its ability to make adjustments. That was the condition of conquering a virgin continent. The majority of us recognize a fact when we hit one, and move over. We have adjusted to the profound changes since 1929 with almost no violence except to our feelings. We are adaptable, and because we are adaptable we are strong.

As a democratic people we have made some grave decisions in recent years. Some of those decisions seemed dead wrong to many sincere and intelligent people, but we recognize the will of the majority, and most of us take off our coats and in good will pitch in to make those decisions effective. We are ready and able to show the world that we are a people firm in our faith in each other and in our democratic precepts.

We can boast that in the United States we have created the most glorious concepts of the objects of human society that any people has ever dedicated itself to:

. . . Life, Liberty and the pursuit of Happiness,
. . . government of the people, by the people, for the people . . .
We hold these truths to be self-evident, that all men are created equal . . .
. . . One nation, indivisible, with liberty and justice for all.

There is no need in America for the slogans of other lands when on our banner are inscribed such imperishable cries of the human spirit as these. A people who can produce and fight for these concepts is a people that can't be beat.

We have great visions today. We are going to have more of them. From our strengths have come great actions. We can move forward to even greater achievements. In our hearts we know we have heard only the opening bars of the New World Symphony.

Ours is a time of great expectations in the face of unprecedented destruction. There is open before us an unparalleled opportunity to build new and firmer foundations under our feet. We stand at the gateway of

an age of expansion, of the flowering of modern imagination and the new skills and knowledge of mankind.

The task ahead may prove to be the boldest and most
stirring adventure of the human spirit since the circum-
navigation of the globe. That will be true if it can release a flood of pent-up genius, not alone in our works
of hand and skills in management but in the development of the free spirit.

What I have in mind in such an era of American
development is not an ideal world lying somewhere in
the remote future, peopled by a different kind of human
beings than we now are, or living under an imaginary
social system. I am speaking of something that can be
done with tools of understanding and organization already ours. I have in mind that reservoir of knowledge
that gives us in our time the power to mold the very
face of things.

The necessary skills of organization and technology
exist today, but this is not to say that it is automatic or
inevitable that they will be used for an age of creation.
We must have the will to set out boldly on the adventure,
the resolution to begin from where we are. We need the
will and the faith, we need a sense that *this* is the historic
hour to turn the first shovel, to take the first steps.

Lack of knowledge does not stand in our way, nor lack
of physical resources. Nor do we want for initiative,
daring, high spirits. The arts of technology and organization, resources and the imaginative spirit are all here.

But there is a not inconsiderable hazard that we may
be sidetracked by disputes among ourselves over eco-

nomic theories and political dogmas. There is some danger that we will let our driving vitality be consumed in controversy over labels such as "reactionary" or "free enterprise," "collectivism" or "radical." Preoccupation with slogans and tags of this sort may divert us from the flesh-and-blood realities that most of us could agree should be done, and can be done to strengthen the basis of democratic life for all Americans.

An American Development Program for the period from 1950 to 1975 can be stated in terms of real things—of land, streams, electricity, forests, minerals; of factories and jobs. A program for America's building that deals with them can be understood and can be acted upon.

America's soil badly needs to be strengthened, the topsoil preserved, the fertility restored, in an intensive twenty-to-thirty-year enterprise. Advances have been made by the farmers and farm agencies of the country in the past three decades. They are only a beginning.

This vast undertaking will vitalize the private business of farming and add to its attractiveness as a family way of life. It will mean new opportunities, new jobs in factories making soil chemicals, agricultural machinery, electric pumps, tractors, materials for millions of farm buildings and rural schools.

America's rivers grievously need to be put under control and made to work for rather than against people. Our technical methods of managing most of our rivers, after decades of effort and billions of dollars of expenditure, are still in the ox-team epoch compared with American progress in nearly every other technical field.

To develop our rivers and control and make them useable by modern methods is by no means beyond our capacities. It will, however, be the largest engineering project of all time. It will save thousands of communities and farms and private businesses from periodic invasion by flood waters. Enterprise will be nourished along the new water highways. Modernized rivers will provide a huge source of electrical energy out of waters now wasted and giving vent to destruction. Irrigation from stored waters will cause millions of acres to flourish that now are fertile but dead. The impounded waters will create spots of beauty for outdoor recreation.

The development of America's watersheds on a huge scale will raise up a profession of great builders. As by-products of their labors would come increased activity in new and existing private undertakings—shipyards for barges and tow boats, electric furnaces, and a hundred other kinds of new and old enterprises. Hotels and hostels for recreation will rise along the new man-made lakes. New highways and airlines and railroads will be called for to keep abreast of the resulting expansion.

After the drain of a century, America's forests need to be restored and refreshed by the most extensive reforestation in human history. On the one hand, this should comprehend the spread of scientific tree culture and harvesting, and an intensive educational effort the country over. On the other, our present forest supplies need to be converted to countless new products made possible by scientific discoveries.

America's minerals call for an exploratory and research

program on a quarter-century schedule, to promote the most prudent and wealth-creating utilization of these fundamental resources.

These programs for forests and minerals would require the training of technicians and administrators of many kinds that would strain universities, private laboratories, and training centers. Hundreds of new industrial processes would throw open interesting new jobs.

These then are real things to be developed and built upon. When one stands in the shadow of New York's magnificent skyscrapers one is likely to forget that their foundation is not the rock of Manhattan but the soil of America and her forests and streams and minerals. This is quite as easy to forget in Omaha in sight of the Great Plains. There is something about being in a city that cuts one off from the underpinnings of our life.

The American Development I am describing is *not* what is usually called "public works." Such would be involved, of course, for bridges and highways and new post offices and schools and sewer systems would be necessary if America struck out on such a program. But that would be incidental. Nor am I proposing schemes of work relief as a "shot in the arm" to tide over the inevitable periods of sag when private employment and investment tend to stagnate. If we fail to strengthen and develop the basic foundations of voluntary undertakings by some such program, we will probably need frequent doses of all kinds of economic benzedrine. The program

I speak of relates not to such measures, whatever their merits, but to the very springs of productiveness itself.

The dogmatist delights in phrases that only confuse, neatly segregating "public" works from "private" enterprise as if they were not both parts of the same living tissue of community existence, interacting and wholly interdependent. Such a worshiper of words may be defined as a man who has his feet firmly planted in mid-air. But new factories and new power plants, new jobs and new products, enriched soil and improved nutrition, the things people want, the things such a building program for the coming generation will produce are realities. They do not rest in midair, like dogmas, but upon firm earth, upon the resources of nature and the technical and organizing skills of men and women.

The expansion in our standard of living in America that can take place between 1950 and 1975 can be accomplished without change in our institutions of government or of property. To do this particular job the Constitution of the United States needs no amendment. The scope and functions of government require no basic revision.

The price citizens would have to pay for such a mammoth building enterprise would not be dictation by private organizations nor coercion by laws. On the contrary, it calls for further development of characteristic American initiative. It depends upon public understanding and cooperation in what is being done by the businessman and the labor leader, by the factory worker and the farmer, by teacher and preacher and librarian and physician and local official. The undertaking is too broad and its threads are too closely interwoven to be possible of accomplishment except by methods that are predominantly voluntary. Were it otherwise, freedom and opportunity for individual development may have lost ground rather than gained it; and consequently the physical achievements would be of dubious value.

The job itself, that is, aiding in the development of natural resources, has been considered an appropriate function of the Federal government for a long, long time. Lake Erie is one of our natural resources; the development of a harbor at federal expense to make that resource more useful is something that the Federal government has been doing over a long period of years. The development of the Ohio River for navigation is another example. The work of the Department of Agriculture in the interest of farming in many states and of forestry, and the work of the Department of Interior in the field of minerals and wildlife and parks are familiar enough the country over. These familiar activities have been paid for, not by the people directly benefited alone, but by the taxpayers of the whole country. Taxpayers in Cleveland and Pasadena, for example, help pay for federal expenditures in the New York harbor or along the Mississippi River or in the agricultural development of Idaho and Arkansas or the forests of Wisconsin and Michigan. The sound theory behind all these federal expenditures in the development of natural resources is that wise and productive expenditures in the development of natural resources in one part of the country benefit the whole country and all the people in it. Handicaps on a region's productiveness will be felt first by the region itself, and to that extent they are regional problems. But they will also be painfully felt by the country as a whole. The healthy, natural development of every region is required for national prosperity.

We think of America today more than ever before not as a group of sections but as a nation. We are in truth one people and we realize that our country cannot be at the zenith of its strength if any one of the great regions that compose it is moving toward the precipice of poverty or the bankruptcy of its resources, or if its people are weighted down by a feeling of hopelessness and despair.

It is what men and women do with the natural resources of their community, their valley, their country that so largely determines their future, whether in the valley of the Missouri or the valley of the Tennessee, whether on the Amazon in Brazil, the Yangtze in China, the Volga, the Danube.

These resources, combined with the skill and enterprise and imagination and faith of men and women, constitute all we have to work with. In any region the world over it is the natural resources of that region and the skill and understanding and hard work of its people upon which human aspirations and opportunities for the flourishing of individual personality depend.

We should know our country's resources and our region's. These are the real things upon which our life is built. We should keep in mind how the United States is put together, what really makes it tick. We should get the interesting habit of looking at a river, for example, as a force in the life of a region rather than a piece of scenery, or the place where people are driven out by floods, communities disrupted, railroads stopped. We should think of floods as waste—waste that properly designed dams could save—and the relation of such dams to factories and farms.

We should begin to look at the land as a vital force that determines the livelihood of our city. We should break through statistics, economic principles, political policies, to the communities which produce lumber and steel, wheat and cattle, and think about their relation to our own field of work and our region.

The kind of American development I have outlined will depend upon all of us. It will depend on our thinking and uttering, almost lovingly, words that speak of pine and cedar, of streams and turbines, of aircraft factories and steel billets; of coal and copper ore; of red clay and black loam and fields of wheat, wave after wave; of river barges and electric power lines; of construction workers and miners, woodsmen and farmers, doctors and teachers—of things and of people. The outcome turns upon whether ours is a static nation resting on its laurels, holding fearfully to what we have or a land which forever renews its youth by magnificent dreams and noble plans turned into great deeds.

Set in Linotype Baskerville
Format by A. W. Rushmore
Manufactured by Knickerbocker Printing Corp., N. Y.
Published by HARPER & BROTHERS, *New York*